Churches respond to
BEM

Churches respond to BEM

Official responses to the "Baptism, Eucharist and Ministry" text

Vol. VI

Edited by Max Thurian

Faith and Order Paper 144
World Council of Churches, Geneva

The text of the United German Mennonite Congregations was translated by Gerhard Bergen.
The WCC Language Service translated the following texts: Slovak Evangelical Church of
the Augsburg Confession in the CSSR, Evangelical Church in Berlin-Brandenburg (West
Berlin), European Continental Province of the Moravian Church, and the Swiss Protestant
Church Federation.

Cover design: Michael Dominguez

ISBN 2-8254-0919-7

© 1988 WCC Publications, World Council of Churches,
150 route de Ferney, 1211 Geneva 20, Switzerland

Printed in Switzerland

CONTENTS

PREFACE

Our documentation series *Churches Respond to BEM* is coming to a provisional end with this sixth volume. However it is a "provisional" end, because the "Baptism, Eucharist and Ministry" process is continuing in many places and there may still be more official responses from churches arriving in our Geneva office. In addition we are still expecting a few translations of responses written in German. Thus a final volume will be necessary by the middle of 1988.

In this volume we have included a few responses not only from churches but also, as we have done before, from councils of churches and individuals.[1] The reason for this is to document reactions and reflections to BEM from such countries where no church or only one church has sent a response. For the first time the Roman Catholic Church has officially responded to an ecumenical document and we are happy to include the response of this church to BEM.

The series *Churches Respond to BEM* is a unique and most important documentation in view of the ecumenical thinking and perspectives of the churches. Nothing comparable has been available thus far. This is another major aspect of the ecumenically very significant and still ongoing BEM process.

This volume has again been edited by my colleague, Frère Max Thurian, and has been prepared for publication by our colleagues in WCC Publications. I am grateful for their untiring collaboration in this large publication project.

Geneva, October 1987   GÜNTHER GASSMANN, Director
                                        WCC Faith and Order Secretariat

---

[1] These responses are published here in the form in which they were received.

INTRODUCTION:
A LETTER TO THE CHURCHES

Dear Sisters and Brothers in Christ,

Five and a half years have passed since the Faith and Order Commission of the World Council of Churches (WCC) adopted its convergence statement on "Baptism, Eucharist and Ministry" (BEM) in Lima/Peru, in January 1982. During this time the Lima statement, usually referred to in the churches as BEM, has become the most widely discussed document in modern ecumenical history. About 350,000 copies have been circulated all over the world in 35 languages — and more translations are still in the making. More than 160 churches have already presented their official responses to BEM to our Faith and Order office in Geneva. These include several churches and communities which are not members of the WCC, such as the Roman Catholic Church which is, however, officially represented on the Faith and Order Commission. Thousands of people in churches, schools, Bible study groups and various ecumenical consultations, meetings and gatherings, have responded to the text on various levels in a boundless variety of ways. We have indeed witnessed an "ecumenical event" in our time of unexpected and unprecedented proportions.

At its meeting in January of this year, the Central Committee of the WCC adopted the recommendation "that the Central Committee:
a) express its appreciation and gratitude to member churches for their active and constructive participation in the BEM process and for their official responses;
b) encourage the member churches to continue the process of discussion and reception of the BEM document;
c) urge the member churches to consider seriously, as far as their ecclesiology permits, the implications of their participation in the BEM process for their own life as well as for their ecumenical relations;

d) ask all member churches which have not yet responded to the BEM document to do so as soon as possible;
e) urge the Faith and Order Commission to continue work on BEM and the responses to it with all their different emphases as a fundamental concern for the whole ecumenical movement and in view of the next Assembly, and to present to the member churches before the coming Assembly a report which offers an evaluation of the responses of the churches."

We are able to report at this time that the BEM process has already had an impact on the thinking and life of many churches in a variety of ways. Teachings and practices are tested in the churches as they engage BEM's presentation of Christian tradition. New ecumenical contacts and relationships are initiated in this process. Liturgical usages are effected in some churches with direct reference to the Lima statement. Several bilateral dialogues and church union negotiations use BEM as a frame of reference for their own reflections. Churches are indicating in their responses concrete implications which the BEM process is having for their own life as well as for their ecumenical relations.

All responses underline the great ecumenical importance of the BEM document, and many of them are able to affirm large sections of the text. Critical comments and suggestions concern mainly basic perspectives of ecclesiology, the relation of scripture and Tradition, the concept of sacramentality and aspects of the understanding and structure of ordained ministry. These and other issues continue to be raised and debated as even now new study materials are in preparation. Seminars on BEM continue to be held in theological schools. New groups are beginning reflections on BEM, and some official responses are still in preparation.

We are still receiving official church responses to BEM. The Commission expects to publish the responses from the churches in six or seven volumes, *Churches Respond to BEM* (WCC, Geneva, 1986-88). We would emphasize the appeal of the Central Committee to those churches which have not yet made their official response to do so as soon as possible. The churches are also encouraged to find ways to evaluate the responses together with us.

Several churches have found it difficult to respond to BEM not only because of the lack of translations, but also because the form and style of the Lima statement is not that with which they are used to work. We are confident that such difficulties will be overcome, and that these churches will make their necessary contribution.

The Standing Commission on Faith and Order wishes to express its gratitude to the churches which have responded to BEM. These responses provide us with the most extensive and representative documentation of the thinking and practice of the churches not only in relation to baptism, eucharist and ministry, but also in relation to their basic ecumenical attitudes and perspectives. The Commission will present a detailed report of the BEM process including a report on the official responses of the member churches at the forthcoming Assembly of the WCC in 1991. We are presently preparing this report for discussion at our next Plenary Commission meeting in August 1989. The report will describe the BEM process, the degree of affirmation and the major critical comments in relation to the different parts of BEM and the more general reflections as well as the specific suggestions made in the responses. In addition we will take a number of critical points and offer some clarification and comments on them as a first step in the continuation of our common work. We will also, of course, be including the findings of the BEM process in our ongoing projects "Towards the Common Expression of the Apostolic Faith Today" and "The Unity of the Church and the Renewal of Human Community".

"Baptism, Eucharist and Ministry" has become an integral part of the current ecumenical movement and an impetus for renewal, mission and growth in Christian community. We are sincerely grateful to you for having accepted our efforts to serve the churches. We commend our work to the Triune God to whose saving purpose for all humanity we dedicate our common service. May the Lord bless and strengthen the churches and the Faith and Order Commission as we continue our common pilgrimage together.

Madrid, Spain   FAITH AND ORDER STANDING COMMISSION
August 1987

ROMAN CATHOLIC CHURCH

Editor's note

The process *for arriving at this response was coordinated by the Secretariat for Promoting Christian Unity.* The process included, first, *consultation starting in 1982 with Catholic episcopal conferences throughout the world, many of which sent reports on BEM to the Secretariat.* Secondly, *reports on BEM received from episcopal conferences and those received from Catholic theological faculties and societies, and other sources, were analyzed and taken into account by the Secretariat for Promoting Christian Unity with the help of a team of theological consultants who worked to develop a draft response to BEM.* Thirdly, *the draft response was brought to its present and final form as a result of collaboration between the Secretariat and the Congregation for the Doctrine of the Faith.*

The Catholic response was sent by the Secretariat for Promoting Christian Unity to the Faith and Order Secretariat in Geneva, in August 1987.

I. INTRODUCTION

Appreciation

The Faith and Order document "Baptism, Eucharist and Ministry" (BEM) has emerged as a culmination of more than fifty years of work that began with the first world conference on Faith and Order held at Lausanne in 1927. The Faith and Order movement is a founding component of the modern ecumenical movement, the search for the restoration of unity

---

● 851,953,000 members, 2,522 dioceses, 3,978 bishops, 212,021 parishes, 403,480 priests (statistics of 31 December 1985).

among all Christians which the Second Vatican Council described as a movement "fostered by the grace of the Holy Spirit",[1] and was one of the paths leading to the formation of the World Council of Churches in 1948. The Faith and Order Commission within the World Council guides the direction of the Faith and Order movement. BEM is perhaps the most significant result of the movement so far.

BEM is significant for several reasons. The first is the nature of the Commission that produced it at Lima in 1982. It consisted of Anglicans, Orthodox, Protestants and Roman Catholics. (Although the Roman Catholic Church is not a member of the World Council of Churches, it officially designates twelve Catholic members to the Commission on Faith and Order who participate, by personal title, as full voting members in the Commission. They constitute one-tenth of the Commission, which has 120 members.) The Commission represents a broad range of churches and communities, "a rich diversity of cultural backgrounds and traditions" who "worship in dozens of languages and live under every kind of political system" (preface to BEM). This Commission claimed to have achieved in BEM "a remarkable degree of agreement", if not yet full consensus, "major areas of theological convergence", while identifying "disputed issues in need of further research and reconciliation" (preface). Theologians coming from groups that were historically often in direct theological confrontation and disagreement with each other, now together claimed agreement and/or convergence on key areas of faith. This itself is a remarkable achievement.

Secondly, BEM is a primary result of the ecumenical process which has been working, in light of the historical background of divisions among Christians, towards the goal of unity in faith. It claims a degree of agreement, or at least areas of theological convergence, which would be an important contribution to this goal. Pope John Paul II told a working group of Faith and Order dealing with BEM in Rome, in 1980, before the final formulation of the document: "Your... persevering effort has already obtained results for which we thank him who is given to us to guide us in the whole truth (cf. John 16:13). It is necessary to continue. It is necessary to reach the goal."[2]

Thirdly, BEM is significant because with it Faith and Order is challenging churches and communities to respond. Having gone through a notable evolution over decades, the Lima text of 1982 was considered mature enough within the limits defined to be sent to the churches and

---

[1] *Unitatis Redintegratio*, n.1.
[2] Secretariat for Promoting Christian Unity, *Information Service*, No. 45, 1981/1.

communities for "official response... at the highest appropriate level of authority" with suggestions given in support of a process of reception. The Sixth Assembly of the World Council of Churches endorsed this proposal and recommended to the churches a timetable within which they might respond. Thus began a phase in the ecumenical movement which signals deeper involvement on the part of Christians in all communities in the task of working for unity.

The Catholic Church and BEM

The Catholic Church sees BEM in relation to important issues that *Unitatis Redintegratio* pointed to in its own elaboration of ecumenical priorities. For one thing the urgent need for unity among divided Christians is expressed by the Vatican Council and also in BEM. A principal concern of the Second Vatican Council was the "restoration of unity among all Christians". The division among Christians, the Council said, "openly contradicts the will of Christ, scandalizes the world and damages that most holy cause, the preaching of the Gospel to every creature" (*UR* 1). The Council noted God's initiative who "in recent times... has begun to bestow more generously upon divided Christians remorse over their divisions and longing for unity". *Unitatis Redintegratio* was formulated by the Second Vatican Council to encourage Catholics to "respond to the grace of this divine call" (*UR* 1). The preface of BEM, for its part, states that "the goal of visible church unity" is what the churches and communities in the World Council of Churches are striving for. Catholics and other Christians may well differ on the conception of what the unity of the church entails, and this must therefore be a matter for ecumenical dialogue. But the common ground here is that, in both cases, there is focus on the urgency of Christian unity. Though not involved in the initial stages of the process within the Faith and Order movement leading to BEM (yet becoming directly involved in the process after the Second Vatican Council), the Catholic Church sees in BEM a significant result of the ecumenical movement. For this reason, it must give the document serious attention.

Unitatis Redintegratio called for ecumenical dialogue (4), pointed to the ecumenical significance of baptism and urged that "the doctrine about the Lord's Supper, about the other sacraments, worship and ministry in the church, should form subjects of dialogue" (22). BEM deals directly with these concerns. *Unitatis Redintegratio* furthermore urged that: "Before the whole world let all Christians confess their faith in God, one and three, in the incarnate Son of God, our Redeemer and Lord" (12). A number of Catholic reactions to BEM have praised the Trinitarian and Christological emphasis given in the text.

Status of the text

Even though we think that the text falls short at certain points, we believe that if it were accepted by the various churches and ecclesial communities, it would bring the churches to an important step forward in the ecumenical movement, although still only one stage along the way in the ecumenical process of working towards visible unity of divided Christians. If through this process of response and reception for BEM, now being undertaken, many of the convergences, even agreements reported by BEM were affirmed by the churches and ecclesial communities, we believe that this would be an advance in the ecumenical movement.

BEM is also *a stage along the way*, one of the "various stages" the churches will have to pass through on "their way towards their goal of visible unity" (preface). Its claims therefore are limited: "We have not yet fully reached 'consensus'... Full consensus can only be proclaimed after the churches reach the point of living and acting together in unity." The text does not offer a full systematic treatment of baptism, eucharist, or ministry, but focuses rather on those aspects which have been related to the problems of mutual recognition leading to unity. It is also formulated with the help of a new theological vocabulary which necessarily includes a new horizon of thought. At important junctions of the document, contrasting statements and language open the way to a variety of interpretations. The commentaries related to the text identify disputed issues still in need of further research and reconciliation. And there are occasional passages which suggest options in theology and practice not consistent, for example, with the Catholic faith.

Contributing to a continuing process

Thus, in responding to BEM, we seek both to identify and acknowledge the achievement, the forward steps that have been taken thus far, and at the same time to see ourselves participating in a process which must continue towards the goal of the visible unity of Christians. The limitations of the document also limit the scope of our response. But we wish to affirm the process and to see it continue to flourish.

In this response we deal with a number of questions which we consider especially important in the text. There is much that we can affirm, and we must build on these positive achievements. There are points that we criticize and these will be clearly noted. There are also some basic issues that we consider critical and in need of further treatment in order to foster continuing progress in the ecumenical movement. But we do not comment on every point in BEM.

Catholic ecclesiological self-understanding

Furthermore in this response we do not speak at length or elaborate on the full Catholic ecclesiological self-understanding (cf. e.g. *Lumen Gentium*). This is because our scope here is more limited, indeed related to the limited scope and content of BEM itself. It is important that this be understood in order to prevent misunderstandings. This response is made in full awareness of the Catholic Church's own unity and truth and without denying what is essential to its self-understanding. We believe, as *Unitatis Redintegratio* states (n. 4), that the "unity of the one and only Church which Christ bestowed on his Church from the beginning... subsists in the Catholic Church as something she can never lose, and we hope that it will continue to increase until the end of time".

It is our conviction that the study of ecclesiology must come more and more into the centre of the ecumenical dialogue. Perhaps the best reflection on BEM will only come after ecclesiology is given more serious attention in the ecumenical dialogue. At the same time, the study of BEM is already a way of dealing with essential realities of the church. But the fact that one does not find a commentary or reflection here relating to every important aspect of Catholic ecclesiological self-understanding should not be interpreted to mean that whatever is not commented on is not important or less significant. It simply means that the focus of this study is not ecclesiology as such. Rather we believe that better attention and clearer understanding would be given to some crucial issues of Catholic ecclesiological self-understanding if they are elaborated within the study of ecclesiology itself. For example, the fundamental Catholic doctrine that the church of Christ "subsists in the Catholic Church"[3] can be truly understood only in the framework of a Roman Catholic ecclesiology of communion.

It is clear to us then that Faith and Order must focus more directly on ecclesiology. We believe that, without serious attention to the broader questions of ecclesiology, there are disadvantages not only for the study and understanding of the content of BEM, but for our ecumenical progress as well.

---

[3] *Lumen Gentium* 8.

A broader ecumenical context

Finally, we appreciate the fact that BEM must be seen within a broader ecumenical perspective. The Nairobi Assembly of the World Council of Churches in 1975 described the unity we seek as a "conciliar community of local churches truly united". Within this context, baptism, eucharist and ministry are some of the fundamental elements of a local church truly united. Ministry, for example, must be seen as an important factor linking local churches as well as an essential means of unity for the local church.

II. THE ONGOING WORK OF FAITH AND ORDER

In order to contribute to building on the solid work already done by Faith and Order, as reflected in much of the BEM text, which we will point to in this response, we wish to state at the outset some critical issues which we see in need of ongoing work by Faith and Order. As we reflect on the text, we think that many of the criticisms that can be raised about it relate to the notions of sacrament (and sacramentality), the precise nature of the apostolic tradition, and the issue of decisive authority in the church. All of these are part of the question of ecclesiology which must be an ongoing concern within the ecumenical movement. We present them to Faith and Order as items that need further treatment. We expect that other insights on the value of the presentation of the three sacraments considered in BEM will emerge when further work is done, in an ecumenical setting, on ecclesiology.

Sacrament and sacramentality

We can speak in positive terms of many things said in the treatment of the sacramental aspect of baptism, eucharist and ministry in BEM. There are many areas of convergence.

Still, we believe that there is an absence of a clear concept of sacrament (and sacramentality) in BEM. Further work is needed on this.

In the text on baptism, for example, the commentaries to 12 and 14 suggest this difficulty. Despite many important points made about the meaning of baptism, there seems to be lack of clarity as well on the full effect of baptism. The text does not give reasons to show clearly why baptism is an unrepeatable act. Is baptism necessary for salvation?

Questions about baptism and initiation into the church are raised here. What are the full dimensions of Christian initiation? Does baptism itself adequately sacramentalize the full reality of Christian initiation? We believe that further study is needed on confirmation as a sacrament. The relationship between baptism and the eucharist needs further exploration as well (cf. B.Comm. 14).

Concerning the text on the eucharist, while there is again a great deal we affirm positively, we also point to areas that we think need clarification and development. For example, concerning the real presence, the description of the change that takes place in the eucharist (cf. E15) is ambiguous and open to several interpretations. The terminology used in the text in regard to the eucharist as sacrifice raises questions about the adequacy of the treatment of this aspect.

Concerning ministry, we think that an important convergence has been achieved because we believe that the description of ordination is such as to point in the direction of a sacramental understanding. But the description is not able fully to reflect the faith of those Christians (including Catholics) for whom ordination is clearly a sacrament. Therefore we believe that further exploration is necessary here.

On the notion of sacrament, BEM shows that there are many aspects that Christians can affirm together. But, because of the importance of seeking agreement on baptism, eucharist and ministry as a step towards Christian unity,[4] we believe that the ongoing work of Faith and Order must include a further and deeper ecumenical exploration of the notion of sacrament and sacramentality.

Apostolic tradition

The precise nature of apostolic tradition and its implications need further attention as well. Surely, within the ecumenical movement the world conference on Faith and Order at Montreal in 1963 was a landmark in providing a way to get beyond the controversies over scripture and Tradition that had marked Catholic/Protestant relationships since the Reformation. In many ways BEM is the beneficiary of the Montreal conference. Still, certain points that are made, particularly in the commentaries in BEM, raise questions about the notion of the apostolic Tradition currently understood by the different churches and ecclesial communities, suggesting that more work has to be done ecumenically on this question.

According to Catholic teaching[5] sacred Tradition and sacred scripture make up a single sacred deposit of the word of God which is entrusted to the church. They are bound closely together. Sacred scripture is the

---

[4] Cf. *Gathered for Life*, Geneva, WCC, 1983, pp.45ff.
[5] Second Vatican Council, *Dei Verbum* 7-10.

speech of God as it is put down in writing under the inspiration of the Holy Spirit. Tradition transmits in its entirety the word of God which has been entrusted to the apostles by Christ, in whom the entire revelation of God is summed up, and the Holy Spirit. It transmits it to the successors of the apostles so that, enlightened by the Spirit of truth, they may faithfully preserve, expound and spread it abroad by their preaching. By adhering to it, the church remains always faithful to the teaching of the apostles, and to the gospel of Christ.

Thus, in our view there must be a clear distinction made between the apostolic tradition, which obliges us because it is rooted in Revelation, and the various traditions which may develop in local churches.

To illustrate the problem, BEM calls to our attention the practice of certain African churches which confer baptism without water (cf. B. Comm. 21). It notes that in certain parts of the world, where bread and wine are not customary or obtainable, it is now sometimes held that local food or drink serve better to anchor the eucharist in everyday life (E. Comm. 28). Perhaps most clearly the difference is seen in relationship to different views on the ordination of women. Commentary 18 of the ministry document notes that those communities which practise ordination of women do so because of their understanding of the gospel, a theological conviction which is said to be reinforced by their experience during the years in which they have included women in their ordained ministries. On the other hand, those which do not ordain women consider that "the force of nineteen centuries of tradition must not be set aside". Is it not obvious that there are different conceptions here of the apostolic tradition and what it implies for an issue such as the ordination of women? We believe therefore that further study and clarification must be done on the precise nature of apostolic tradition, as Faith and Order continues its important task.

Authority in the church

Further study is also needed on the nature of authority in the church. Within an ecumenical context, this concern was raised again at the Sixth Assembly of the World Council of Churches at Vancouver in 1983. Besides proposing BEM for response and reception, another of the steps towards unity recommended by Vancouver was that of furthering "the Church's common quest for agreement on common ways of decision-making and teaching authoritatively".[6]

---

[6] *Gathered for Life*, *op. cit.*, p.50.

A number of questions on authority are raised for us by the BEM text. What are the constitutive elements of authority and order in the church? What is the nature and role of decisive authority in the discernment of God's will as to the development of ministry in the church in the past and with regard to the present needs of the church? Related to this is the precise understanding of the threefold ministry and its functions, as presented in BEM. For example, according to the BEM text, does the threefold ministry belong to the constitutive being of the church as rooted in God's will for the church, or only to the ecumenical wellbeing (bene esse) of the church? How is this decided? With what authority?

Concerning episcopal succession, when it is said that it is a "sign" of continuity and unity in the church (M38), what does "sign" mean here? What is the ecclesiological meaning of the episcopal succession for ordination? What is the precise difference and relationship between the priesthood of all, and the priesthood of the ordained? What are the ecclesiological dimensions of the authority of the ordained minister? Further study must be done on the fundamental ecclesiological aspects of the question of the recognition of ministry. The recognition of ordained ministry and the ecclesial character of a church community are indissolubly and mutually related. And should not the question of a universal ministry in the church be explored? By what authority are such questions decided?

We would encourage Faith and Order to undertake the suggestion of the Vancouver Assembly mentioned above, and to study the question of authority in the church. The nature of authority in the church is a key for the progress of ecumenism.

III. BEM AND THE FAITH OF THE CHURCH

We turn to a more particular reflection on the text in relationship to the "faith of the church through the ages" (preface). There is a great deal that we affirm in the text, while noting difficulties as well.

A. Baptism

1. GENERAL APPRECIATION

We find the text on baptism to be grounded in the apostolic faith received and professed by the Catholic Church. It draws in a balanced way from the major New Testament areas of teaching about baptism; it gives an important place to the witness of the early church. While it does not discuss all major doctrinal issues that have arisen about baptism, it is sensitive to the effect they have had on the development of the under-standing of this sacrament and to the positive values of differing solutions that emerged; it appreciates the normative force that some forms of liturgical celebration may have and the significance of pastoral practice; within the ecumenical scope it sets for itself, it articulates the develop-ment of the Christian understanding of baptism with a coherent theologi-cal method. It has many affinities, both of style and of content, with the way the faith of the church about baptism is stated in the Second Vatican Council and in the *Liturgy of Christian Initiation* promulgated by Pope Paul VI.[7]

The faith of the church is well stated on the following matters:

a) Baptism is confessed to be the gift and work of the Trinitarian God (1,7,17). Faith in the Trinity allows the text to deal profoundly with the Christ-centredness of baptism and with the role correspondingly played in it by the Holy Spirit (4,5,7,14).

b) The practice of baptism is an integral part of God's plan to gather all into his kingdom through the church, in which the mission of Christ is continued through the Spirit (1,7,10).

c) Baptism is a sacramental reality. The text calls baptism a sacrament (23 and Comm. 13). But it deals with the question, not so much by using the word (which, because of its complex history, needs a great deal of explanation in interchurch conversations) as by affirming the principal features of baptism that the word sacrament has served to express. It says:

— Baptism is a sign (2,18), with definite ritual requirements (17,20), celebrated in and by the church (12,22,23); it is a sign of the faith of the church (12), of its faith in Christ and in the new life that he inaugurated in his paschal mystery (2,3,4), of its faith in the gift of the Holy Spirit in whom this life is shared (5).

— Participation in Christ's death and the gift of the Holy Spirit are both signified and effected by baptism (14).

— The effective sign that is baptism was inaugurated by Jesus (1).

— Baptism is both God's gift to us and our human response to that gift (8). The gift that it signifies and effects is the washing away and overcoming of sin (2,3), conversion, pardon and justification (3,4), incorporation into Christ (6), moral sanctity (4) of which the Holy Spirit is the source and seal (5), the making of men and

---

[7] Cf. *SC* 6, *LG* 4 and 10, *UR* 22; *Christian Initiation, General Introduction* 1-6, *Initiation of Adults* 8, *Initiation of Children* 2-3.

women to be sons and daughters of God in Christ the Son (5), who will finally enter their full inheritance to the praise of the glory of God (5). Our response is faith (8), confession of sin and conversion (4), life-long moral effort, under the transforming power of grace, to grow in the likeness of Christ (9), and work for the coming of the kingdom of God on earth as in heaven (7,10).

— Baptism, in making us one with Christ, makes us one with each other and "with the Church of every time and place" (6); it signs and seals us in this common fellowship (6) and is an unrepeatable act (13).

2. PARTICULAR COMMENTS

The institution of baptism

The text is a careful statement of the fundamental truth that is affirmed when baptism is said to have been instituted by Christ. The reality that is symbolized in the rite of baptism is the reality of Christ himself, giving himself in death and resurrection, and being accepted in the way he commanded by those who are called to enter the New Covenant. That baptism is the way he commanded is made known through the apostolic witness found in the scripture and in the Tradition of the church.

The meaning of baptism

Baptism incorporates people into the body of Christ, bringing them into union "with each other and with the Church of every time and place" (6). This is well explained by the text. The document does not here give adequate attention, however, to the implications of the fact that a person is baptized within a particular ecclesial fellowship in a divided Christianity. Because the text is addressed to churches and communities that are not in full communion with one another, it rightly emphasizes that, in uniting people to Christ, baptism establishes a bond between them that is deeper than anything that divides them. It draws attention to the contradiction between one baptism and divided Christian communities, and calls for an overcoming of division and a visible manifestation of baptismal fellowship (6).

When the text speaks of the "dynamic of baptism which embraces the whole of life, extends to all nations, and anticipates the day when every tongue will confess that Jesus Christ is Lord to the glory of God the Father" (7), it touches the question of the relationship between baptism and salvation of all humankind — a question which is also connected with the necessity of the church for salvation. Since the text is dealing with the meaning of baptism, and not with the whole plan of salvation, it is perhaps understandable that it does not say anything about the salvation of those who are not baptized. But neither does the text deal explicitly with the question of the necessity of baptism for salvation, which clearly requires further common study.

The question of the necessity of baptism for salvation is connected with, although not totally dependent on, the development of the doctrine of original sin. The text seems to refer to the reality which the doctrine of original sin expresses in 3 ("By baptism Christians... but free"). Here, as in other passages, the text says clearly that baptism takes away sin, but it does not go into the question of whether or why all are sinners in the way the doctrine of original sin has done.

It is understandable that in a convergence text like this, Faith and Order might prefer to avoid using the term original sin. However, underlying the doctrine of original sin is an understanding in faith about universal human sinfulness, about the universal need for salvation, about Christ as the universal Saviour, and about the necessity of baptism for salvation. It is a doctrine that can claim solid roots in the scriptures (e.g. Rom. 5) and that took shape in the patristic age. It has a profound influence on baptismal doctrine and practice. The faith of the church that it expresses remains obscure in the text. Therefore we think it would be appropriate that the doctrine of original sin, both in name and content, be explicitly incorporated into the discussion on the meaning and effects of baptism.

In dealing with "Incorporation into the Body of Christ" (6), the text says: "Baptism is a sign and seal of our common discipleship." In 5 too, it speaks of the seal with which the baptized are marked. We think that there should be clarification of what is meant here by the "seal". What is the full meaning of the seal? Towards that clarification, we make the following observations.

The image of "seal", especially when taken in conjunction with the liturgical practice of signing and anointing those being baptized with the form of a cross, was much developed in the patristic period. It is not clear if the text is alluding in the passages quoted to these patristic developments. They did not have an important place in the reflection of the church, especially in the Latin tradition, about the sacramentality of baptism. They entered into the explanations of why baptism is not repeated, of how there can be a real sacrament even when, because of lack of due disposition, a baptized person does not seem to live as if he or she were sanctified, of how baptism incorporates people into the church, and of how the baptism in a community that is judged to be out of full communion with the church can still be recognized as a true baptism.

These remain real issues related to baptism. They are not addressed in the text. A theology of the baptismal character, growing out of Augustine's reflection on the seal, does raise and deal with them. An ecumenical rediscovery of the extent to which such a theology represents an important part of the patristic tradition would, we believe, enrich the Lima text on baptism.

Baptism and faith

There is a deep doctrine of grace inherent in the explanation given in 8-10 of how human response meets the gift of God in baptism. The text is an invitation to a deep baptismal spirituality.

On the one hand, it is affirmed that it is God's gift of salvation that is embodied (contained) and set forth (signified) in baptism. On the other hand, it is affirmed that this grace given in baptism calls forth and is received in faith, in commitment to growth in holiness, and in care for the world. This grace is the work of the Holy Spirit. It is given, and creates among those who are baptized a fellowship in faith, in love and "in hope for the manifestation of God's new creation and for the time when God will be all in all" (10). The references to the church in these paragraphs, and particularly the use of the word "context" to describe its role (10), seem, however, less than adequate to express the ecclesiological dimension of baptismal grace.

Baptismal practice

In regard to the section on the "baptism of believers and infants", we appreciate the difficulty of formulating a text which would encompass the beliefs of those who are convinced of the importance of baptism for infants and those who believe that baptism is only justified when the one to be baptized is an adult believer. Keeping in mind what has been said previously concerning original sin, grace, etc., we commend the efforts of Faith and Order for seeking in BEM to clarify the common ground between these positions. But we think that further study is still needed on this issue.

The issue is dealt with on the level of practice. In the sacramental life of the church, practice expresses faith, and the faith is also deepened from reflection on practice. The constant practice of the church is a basic factor that justifies the baptism of infants. At the same time the faith of the church has been ready from the earliest times to answer difficulties that have been raised against the practice, and to provide reasons for continuing it.

The doctrine that a profession of faith is required in baptism is also grounded on liturgical and pastoral practice, primarily in the baptism of adults but also in the baptism of infants. All this is well presented in the text. Particularly good is the explanation of how the reality of baptism is assured, on the one hand, by "Christ's faithfulness unto death" (12) and by "the faithfulness of God, the ground of all life in faith" (*ibid.*); and on the other hand by the response of faith, which is always the faith of the community (12). The text shows how this pattern is fulfilled both in the baptism of those who make a personal profession of faith at the moment of baptism and in those who will be brought to that profession of faith subsequently by Christian nurture. The faith of these latter is seen as a response to "the promise and claim of the Gospel" that has been laid upon them (Comm. 12).

But the terminology used in the text "baptism of believers and infants" requires comment. Baptized infants are incorporated into Christ and are members of the believing community. It follows that the distinction the text seems to make between "infants" and "believers" is misleading. It might have been better if the text spoke of baptism of adults and infants.

The Catholic practice and belief about the importance of the baptism of infants stems from some fundamental convictions of faith about baptism already mentioned in the text. Baptism is first of all a gift of God (cf. 1). It is a gift through which one can participate in the saving mysteries of the life, death and resurrection of Jesus Christ, where the power of sin is broken, and new life with Christ begins (cf. 3). Infants are affected by original sin. But through baptism they share in the new life in Christ. But they must then be brought, through Christian nurture, to that profession of faith. This too is very important. It may be that the concern about apparent "indiscriminate baptism" in 16 stems from a perception on the part of some of those who do not practise it, that infant baptism has been practised in a way that seems "magical" or "automatic", as if there were no concern beyond the act of baptism itself. In fact, there is a serious pastoral responsibility within the church not only for preparation of the baptism of an infant, but also of the Christian nurture which follows. Parents or guardians have the serious responsibility to see to the nurture of baptized children leading to a mature commitment to Christ. Being faithful to this responsibility can also be a contribution towards overcoming differences between the churches and communities which incorporate infants into the community of believers through baptism and those practising only the baptism of adult believers.

Concerning the discussion of "baptism-chrismation-confirmation", 14 is a fair statement of the faith of the church about the gift of the Holy

Spirit in Christian initiation, as it has developed through the ages. It is a complex theological development, as the steps taken by our own church since Vatican II to renew the liturgy, theology and pastoral practice of confirmation testify.

We do, however, believe that the emergence of a distinctive sacramental rite called chrismation or confirmation is a normative development in the faith of the church. While the gift of the Holy Spirit is given in baptism, certain aspects of that Pentecostal gift have come to be effectively symbolized in the liturgy of Christian initiation by anointing with perfumed oil and a prayer with laying on of hands. Among such aspects are its empowerment for witness and for standing firm in trials, and its public manifestation of membership in the church. Some of these have already been mentioned in 5 of the text. An evocation of them here would have opened the way to a better theological understanding of why the Catholic Church believes that chrismation/confirmation is a sacrament distinct from baptism in which there is given a special and unique gift of the Holy Spirit. This is part of the liturgical process of Christian initiation that can stand on its own as a sacramental celebration of the church.

We agree with the statement that "baptism, as incorporation into the body of Christ, points by its very nature to the eucharistic sharing of Christ's body and blood..." (Comm. 14b; cf. *UR* 22). More might have been made of this truth in the main text. It would have helped to clarify certain aspects of baptism, particularly its ecclesiological dimension. Christian initiation begun in baptism is completed by participation in the eucharist, which is the sacrament that engages and manifests the full reality of the church.

We agree with Commentary 14c, that baptism needs to be reaffirmed constantly. We do so in our liturgy in the ways suggested. In reaffirming baptism, the eucharist, of course, also completes it, because it is the fullness of that life towards which baptism is directed. We see confirmation as another step after baptism in the process of initiation, and therefore something that has its own place in developing the life that finds its fullness in the eucharist.

The celebration of baptism

What is said in this section of the text about the celebration of baptism is liturgically rich and includes all of the classical elements related to that celebration. An acceptance of it by ecclesial communities would certainly contribute greatly towards the process of mutual recognition of baptism.

We agree with the concern expressed in Commentary 21a, about integrating the celebration of baptism as much as possible in the culture of those who are being evangelized. Regarding the practice mentioned in Commentary 21c, we note simply that we consider the use of water to be essential for baptism. On a question of fact, we would wonder what kind of evidence there is to support the judgment made in Commentary 21b that "in many large European and North American majority churches infant baptism is often practised in an apparently indiscriminate way".

Thus in the text on baptism we find much we can agree with, as well as points to be studied further in the Faith and Order process.

B. The eucharist

1. GENERAL APPRECIATION

Catholics can recognize in the statement on the eucharist much that corresponds to the understanding and practice of the apostolic faith, or, as it is said in the document, the faith of the church through the ages.

We especially appreciate the following:

a) The sources employed for the interpretation of the meaning of the eucharist and the form of celebration are scripture and Tradition. The classical liturgies of the first millennium and patristic theology are important points of reference in this text.

b) The eucharist is described as pertaining to the content of faith. It presents a strong Christological dimension, identifying the mystery of the eucharist in various ways with the real presence of the risen Lord and his sacrifice on the cross.

c) The structure and ordering of the basic aspects of the document, as well as their relation to one another, conforms with Catholic teaching, specifically:

— The presentation of the mystery of the eucharist follows the flow of classical eucharistic liturgies, with the eucharistic theology drawing heavily on the content of the traditional prayer and symbolic actions of these liturgies. The text draws on patristic sources for additional explication of the mystery of the eucharist.

— There is strong emphasis on the Trinitarian dimension. The source and goal of the eucharist is identified as the Trinity.

— The explanation of the content of the act of the church in the eucharistic prayer includes basic elements required by Catholic teaching as well: thanksgiving to the Father, memorial of the institution of the eucharist and the sacrifice of the cross; intercession made in union with Christ for the world; petition for the Spirit's coming on the bread and wine and on the community, in order that the bread and wine become the body and blood of Christ, and that the community be sanctified; the meal of the New Covenant.

d) There is a strong eschatological dimension. The eucharist is viewed as a foretaste of Christ's parousia and of the final kingdom (6), given through the Spirit (18). It opens up the vision of the kingdom (22) and the renewal of the world (23).

e) The eucharist is presented as the central act of the church's worship (1). Because of this, the text recommends frequent celebration (30).

f) The text has important ecclesiological dimensions (8) and implications for mission.

2. PARTICULAR COMMENTS

The institution of the eucharist

The explanation of the institution of the eucharist accounts for its historical grounding in the life and death of Jesus of Nazareth and also relates it to the risen Lord. In this way it is made clear that the eucharist is not merely a subjective memorial of what Christ did in the past, but relates to the saving mystery of Christ in the life of the church today: the risen Lord, on the basis of his presence (if properly understood), institutional word and the power of the Holy Spirit, is the host and meal of the church.

The text highlights the link between the last supper and the eucharist. The description of the eucharist as "a gift from the Lord", "a sacramental meal", given to the church as a means "to remember and encounter him", and "a sacramental meal which by visible signs communicates to us God's love in Jesus Christ": all this is taught as well by the Catholic Church.

The meaning of the eucharist

The definition of eucharist as "sacrament of the gift which God makes to us in Christ through the power of the Spirit" combines the two aspects of the mystery of the eucharist: the real presence of Christ effected by the Spirit and the gift signified by this. The gift is identified as "salvation" received through communion "in the body and blood" of Christ. Stating that "... in eating and drinking the bread and wine, Christ grants communion with himself", the text shows that Christ is the true host of the meal, the giver of the gift. But, since the gift is himself, the unambiguous biblical language, which speaks of participation of the body and blood of Christ (cf. 1 Cor. 10:16; John 6:52-56) should be used here.

The link between eucharist and forgiveness of sins is grounded on Matthew 26:28. But the "assurance of the forgiveness of sins" through the eucharist is preconditioned by the state of reconciliation with God in the church. This points to the need for previous reconciliation of sinners (cf. 1 Cor. 11:28). In our understanding the previous reconciliation would take place through the sacrament of penance.

In the section on "the eucharist as thanksgiving to the Father", we find that the description of the breadth and depth of the thanksgiving, given in the eucharistic prayer, reflects faithfully the riches of the classical liturgical tradition. But whatever be the historical links between the form of Jewish prayer (*berakah*) that is mentioned[8] and the eucharistic prayer, the latter has a unique trait, which is well expressed in "Eucharist": a thanksgiving for what God has done in the economy of salvation marked by memorial of and founded on the Christ-event.

The thanksgiving of the church is grounded on the one High Priest: "This sacrifice of praise is possible only through Christ, with him and in him" (4). This statement recalls the conclusion of the Roman Canon, which affirms that the eucharistic prayer is first and foremost the thanksgiving of Jesus Christ to the Father. The relation between the act of the church and the act of Christ could be more clearly expressed by stating that the church receives the thanksgiving of Jesus Christ in the eucharist and associates herself with it as bride of Christ in order to express the acceptable thanksgiving of all God's benefits. In the Catholic understanding, the eucharist as thanksgiving signifies above all the thanksgiving of Jesus Christ to the Father, with the offering of his body and blood for the remission of sins and the salvation of the world.

The text in 4 speaks of the bread and wine as a locus for the presence of the world at the eucharist, and as "fruits of the earth", "presented to the Father in faith and thanksgiving". But the identity between the gift which Jesus Christ makes of his life and the sacramental gesture of the church requires that it be made clear that the gifts of bread and wine, the visible expression of what is being celebrated here and now, are the sacramental signs of Christ's presence.

---

[8] Is it appropriate to classify the eucharist as *berakah* or even to explain, as is done in III.27, that it is derived "from the Jewish tradition of the berakah"? At the present stage of investigation of the history of *berakah* and its relation to eucharistic prayers, many questions remain open.

The presentation of the "eucharist as *anamnesis* or memorial of Christ" is well done. The biblical concept of memorial is employed in a precise way. The eucharist is not a mere recalling of a past event. Rather, *anamnesis* is used to express the idea of the effective, operative presence of the sacrifice of the cross in and through the eucharistic celebration, for the benefit "of all humankind". The implied analogy between the eucharist and Old Covenant liturgies is based on "the present efficacy of God's work when it is celebrated by God's people in a liturgy". We find the presentation which stresses the analogy between memorial celebration of Israel and the eucharist acceptable. The differences between the two is expressed in 5-8.

The connection established between the sacrifice of the cross and the eucharist corresponds to Catholic understanding. The sacrifice of the eucharist is one in which the sacrifice of the cross is represented to the end that its saving power be applied here and now for the salvation of the world.

The present efficacy of the sacrifice of the cross in the eucharist is grounded on the presence of the risen Lord who cannot be separated from his saving work (6). He is present "in the *anamnesis*" (commemorative personal presence) as coming from the future to grant communion with himself as "a foretaste of the parousia and of the final kingdom". The traditional belief that Christ is host of the meal from the outset, as well as gift of the meal, comes to the foreground while, at the same time, important ecclesiological aspects of the eucharist are mentioned. The connection between eucharist and the economy of salvation, already realized fully in the ascension of Christ and the blessed in him, is established.

The intimate relation between the mystery content of the eucharist and the activity of the church is succinctly formulated (7). It recalls Catholic theology's presentation of the threefold dimension of sacramental celebrations. Since "Christ acts through the joyful celebration of the Church", the eucharist is "not only a calling to mind of what is past", but "the Church's effective proclamation of God's mighty acts" (a real participation now) and "promises" (a real foretaste of the future glory).

The ecclesiological dimension of the eucharistic doctrine is expressed in the text's theology of intercession: "The eucharist is the sacrament of the unique sacrifice of Christ, who lives to make intercession for us... the Church offers its intercession in communion with Christ, our High Priest" (8). Here the church is seen to be united spiritually and sacramentally to the commemorative active presence of the sacrifice of Christ. In her intercession, the church makes her own the very intercession of Christ himself (cf. Comm. 8). Elsewhere it is said: "It is in the eucharist that the community of God's people is fully manifested. Eucharistic celebrations always have to do with the whole church and the whole church is involved in each local eucharistic celebration" (19). This statement implies an understanding of the mystery of church and eucharist which corresponds to the traditional eucharistic ecclesiology of the Catholic Church.

The eucharist embodies the movement of the church in Christ to the Father. The value of the thanksgiving and intercession of the church is affirmed on the basis of its inclusion in the intercession of Christ (8). This relates to Catholic teaching which expresses the belief that the eucharist is an offering made to the Father by the whole Christ, head and body, in the power of the Holy Spirit.

But at several points (8, Comm. 8,9) the notion of intercession is used in a way that could seem insufficient to explain the sacrificial nature of the eucharist in the Catholic sense. The statement that the eucharist is the "sacrament of the unique sacrifice of Christ" (8) refers to the relationship between the historical sacrifice of the cross and the eucharistic celebration. The link between the historical event of the cross and the present efficacy of that event is the crucified and risen Lord, established as High Priest and "Intercessor". In this perspective it is correct to say that the "events" of Christ's life, as historical events, were caught up in the flow of time and cannot be repeated "or prolonged". But since the High Priest is the crucified and risen Lord, his offering of self on the cross can be said to be "made eternal". His glorified body is the body of the Lord offered once-for-all. Consequently, it does not seem to do justice to the reality of Christ's sacrifice to describe the continuity of Christ's saving work only in terms of simple "intercession".

Correspondingly, the description of the church's activity in the eucharist as thanksgiving and intercession needs to be filled out by some reference to the self-offering of the participants of the eucharist, made in union with the eternal "self-offering" of Christ. Section II, 9-10-11 can be read in such a way that this notion is included.

The suggestion is made (Comm. 8) that Catholic doctrine's references to the eucharist as propitiatory sacrifice be understood in terms of intercession. But Catholics would ask: Is it sufficient to describe the role of Christ, in the "application of the propitiatory effects of the cross", as "intercessor"?

The traditional *anamnesis*-offering prayer expresses the idea that there is an offering of the one acceptable sacrifice made by the church in union with Christ. For Catholics this prayer would express the belief that through the eucharist we are enabled to associate ourselves with the passover of Christ to his Father. A veiled reference to this aspect seems to be found in 9: "In the eucharist, Christ empowers us to live with him, to suffer with him... as justified sinners." But Catholic theology prefers to state more clearly and directly with reference to the eucharist, what is said (in 10) about the spiritual worship offered to God in daily life. But again, the empowerment by Christ is explained only in terms of "intercession" (9). From the Catholic perspective, it might have been good to take more account of Christ's role as sanctifier (cf. previous remarks on 8).

The formulation of, the relation of the preaching of the word to the celebration of the eucharist (12) is correct; it does not confound the preaching of the word with the eucharist; at the same time, it affirms the intimate relation between the two.

We appreciate the presentation in the text of the real presence of Christ. The passages which deal with the relation of the risen Lord to the elements of the eucharist include an appeal not only to the witness of scripture (cf. 13: "the words and acts of Christ at the institution of the eucharist stand at the heart of the celebration"), but also to the *epiklesis* of the liturgy which asks for the coming of the Spirit on the elements (14-15). If it could be interpreted in the light of the implications of the theology of the *epiklesis* of the Spirit, as found in patristic teaching, the presentation satisfies the requirements of Catholic belief. Catholic tradition and practice, we should add here, puts emphasis on the importance of the words of institution within the eucharistic celebration.

The significance of the church's recall on the words and acts (13) of Christ at the institution of the eucharist conforms to the authentic doctrine. "At the heart of the celebration" the church proclaims what Christ did once for all. The risen Lord relates himself to this activity. He places the elements of bread and wine in the relation between himself and the community. These elements are made signs which realize his saving presence, namely, "sacrament of his body and blood". In this way Christ fulfills one of the ways he promised to be "with his own".

The statement about the fact and the mode of Christ's "unique" presence, which "does not depend on the faith of the individual", is adequate. But Catholic faith links the sacrificial aspect of the eucharist to the sacrament of the body and blood more closely than is done in the text. Jesus did not say simply: "This is my body... This is my blood..." According to the New Testament he added: "...body, given for you;... blood, shed for the many". Christ first offered himself sacramentally to the Father in the eucharist, in a sacrifice that actualizes the redemption of humanity. If he now offers himself as a means of sacramental communion to the faithful, it is to allow them to associate themselves with his self-offering to the Father. Only insofar as Christ offers himself to the Father in the sacrificial action of the church's liturgy do the elements become sacrament of his self-offering to the communicants. But, from our view, although the text speaks of the "present efficacy" (5) "of the sacrifice of Christ" (5), and "the living and effective sign of his sacrifice" (5) and the eucharist as the "sacrament of the unique sacrifice of Christ" (8), it does not say unambiguously that the eucharist is in itself a real sacrifice, the memorial of the sacrifice of Christ on the cross.

A distinction is made in Commentary 13 between churches that "believe" in the *change* of the elements and those which do not link Christ's presence "so definitely to the signs of bread and wine". But the final sentence seems to relativize the word "believe". It asks whether the "difference can be accommodated with the convergence formulated in the text itself". On the one hand, we welcome the convergence that is taking place. On the other hand, we must note that for Catholic doctrine, the *conversion* of the elements is a matter of faith and is only open to possible new theological explanations as to the "how" of the intrinsic change. The content of the word "transubstantiation" ought to be expressed without ambiguity. For Catholics this is a central mystery of faith, and they cannot accept expressions that are ambiguous. Thus it would seem that the differences as explained here cannot be accommodated within the convergence formulated in the text itself. Further work must be done on this.

While focusing more on the pneumatological element, this section on "the eucharist as invocation of the Spirit" (14-18) emphasizes the intimate relation between the mystery of the eucharist and the mystery of the Triune God. It sets forth the role of the Father, Son and Holy Spirit in the eucharist in a way that is in conformity with Catholic teaching. The statement that the whole action of the eucharist has an "epicletic" character because it depends on the work of the Holy Spirit (16) is appropriate and emphasizes the fact that the eucharist is a holy work from the outset.

According to the text, the bread and wine are said to "become the sacramental signs of Christ's body and blood" (15) in virtue of the words of Christ and the power of the Spirit. This corresponds to Catholic teaching which also refers to the bread and wine as sacramental signs (*sacramentum tantum*, i.e., insofar as they signify). But the thought that they become sacamental signs is linked to the intrinsic change which takes place, whereby unity of being is realized between the signifying reality and the reality signified. The reference to the sanctifying action of the Spirit weights the statement of the text in the direction of intrinsic change. But the text is also open to the idea that the gifts undergo a change of meaning, which does not go beyond the establishment of an extrinsic relation between the thing signifying and the thing signified. This would be inadequate. Since this matter relates to the important question of the real presence further explanation is needed from the perspective of Catholic faith.[9]

The presentation of "the eucharist as communion of the faithful" gives expression to an important ecclesiological point: "The eucharistic communion with Christ who nourishes the life of the Church is at the same time communion with the body of Christ which is the Church" (19). And in this context it draws out ethical implications of participation in the eucharist, centring on the need to face and overcome divisiveness within the church and in the world.

At the same time, Commentary 19 raises a concern that "the catholicity of the eucharist is less manifest" when "the right of the baptized believers and their ministers to participate in and preside over the eucharistic celebration in one church is called into question by those who preside over and are members of other eucharistic congregations". But the catholicity of the eucharist is not something different from the catholicity of the church. Catholicity includes openness, but an openness conditioned by acceptance of the whole saving mystery of Christ and its consequences. But the issues raised (in Comm. 19) in relationship to it must ultimately be situated within an ecclesiology to be adequately answered.

The explanation of "the eucharist as a meal of the kingdom" suggests a valuable commentary on the link between baptism and eucharist. Through baptism one is justified, incorporated into Christ and ordered to the eucharist (cf. *UR* 22), which is the representation of the saving mystery of Christ under the aspect of the sharing in the eschatological meal of joy with Christ and the blessed into the kingdom, unto the glory of the Father.

The text recalls how the eschatological dimension of the eucharist grounds the mission of the church. The link between eucharist and mission is integral to the Catholic explication of the connection between eucharist and life. Christian ethic has a sacramental basis. Through the

---

[9] Somewhat related to this, the various attempts to understand the mystery of the eucharistic presence of Christ are placed (Comm. 15) at three levels: (1) some affirm only the fact; (2) others "consider it necessary to assert" a change of bread and wine; (3) others develop theological explanations. Catholic theology, which includes all three levels, requires a reformulation of the description of its understanding of the second level. Our faith in the real presence implies that we believe that the bread and wine become really the body and blood of Christ. The phrase "consider it necessary to *assert*" is not adequate to express this. *Consider it necessary to confess* would be more appropriate.

eucharist the church not only receives its name (body of Christ, 24), but also its mission to extend Christ's salvation to the world.

The celebration of the eucharist

In general, the description of the elements of the classical liturgical celebration of the eucharist is adequate. The list of elements includes a "lex orandi" which is able to converge towards a "lex credendi" of the church. But there are some reservations or questions from the standpoint of Catholic doctrine. First, instead of "declaration of pardon", we would prefer to have a phrase that indicates more precisely the element of true forgiveness of sin in the life of the Christian. Secondly, the expression of the church's intention to offer the sacrifice of Christ is important. Is it implied in the listing under "the *anamnesis* or memorial... etc."? This should be clearer. Thirdly, the expression "eating and drinking in communion with Christ and with each member of the Church" is weak. It does not sufficiently express the distinction between sacramental participation of the body and blood of Christ and communion with Christ through communion with those who are in Christ.

The problem of changeable and unchangeable elements of the eucharistic celebration (Comm. 28) is correctly referred to the responsibility of the church. It is the church and not the individual as such that has the assurance of the guidance of the Spirit in this matter. The description of Christ at work in the eucharist is well stated (29). But the question of the president of the eucharist could perhaps be dealt with better in the text on ministry. The Catholic position is that the one who presides must be a priest sacramentally ordained within the apostolic succession.

A distinction is made (32) between churches, which stress "that Christ's presence in the consecrated elements continues after the celebration", and others, which place "the main emphasis on the act of celebration itself and on the consumption of the elements in the act of communion". The Catholic Church agrees with the first position and also agrees with what is said positively about the second position. She only disagrees with those who deny the duration of the real presence after the celebration. And we would ask, if one denies the duration of the real presence after the celebration, what does this signify for one's understanding of real presence and the reality of the conversion? Therefore, it would have been useful to indicate the deeper ecclesiological sacramental and eschatological grounds for the ancient practice of reservation of the consecrated species. While the text states that "the best way of showing respect for the elements... is by the consumption, without excluding the use for communion of the sick", we would add to this that the various forms of eucharistic worship, properly done, are also legitimate and praiseworthy ways of acknowledging the continuing presence of Christ in the eucharist.

Finally, the policies of the churches and ecclesial communities differ in regard to eucharistic sharing. In our view, the problem of eucharistic sharing (33) has an ecclesial dimension and cannot be resolved in isolation from an understanding of the mystery of the church as well as the ministry. In this regard, for Catholics, it is unity in the profession of faith that constitutes the core of ecclesial communion. Because the eucharistic celebration is by its very nature a profession of the faith of the church, it is impossible for the Catholic Church presently to engage in general eucharistic sharing. For in our view we cannot share in the eucharist unless we share fully in that faith.

In the text on the eucharist we find much we can agree with, and have pointed to areas where we believe further study is needed as the Faith and Order process continues.

C. Ministry

1. GENERAL APPRECIATION

The statement on ministry deals with one of the central and most complex themes in ecumenical conversations. We are well aware that perhaps none of the churches or ecclesial communities represented in the Faith and Order Commission can find its faith and practice in regard to ministry fully reflected and stated in this document in precisely the way that it has understood and experienced it. It is necessarily influenced by the variety of views and practices present in the Faith and Order Commission. Furthermore, the ministerial structures of the churches and communities divided from one another are not only marked by differing theologies, but have also been affected by various historical and sociological developments within the churches which contribute heavily to shaping their identity. Well aware of the complexity of the ecumenical dialogue on ministry, we are grateful for the work achieved on it by the Commission and we appreciate especially the fact that its presentation goes in the direction of the major lines of what we recognize "as the faith of the Church through the ages".

In that light we would especially single out:
a) the use within a wider ecumenical horizon of a terminology that reflects traditional Christian theology;
b) the significant Trinitarian, Christological and ecclesiological aspects of the text;

c) the embodiment of the ordained ministry within the wider theological
   and ecclesiological horizon of God's salvific work through Christ and
   his church, in which diverse and complementary gifts are bestowed
   upon the community and the individual members of the whole people
   (Section I);
d) the continuous connection of the ordained ministry with the mission
   of the Twelve and the fundamental apostolicity of the church;
e) the well-balanced description of the ordained ministry as the result of
   God's gratuitous initiative and of a commissioning by the church for a
   responsibility in the church in Christ's name;
f) the positive description of ordination which, although open to
   various interpretations, remains open as well to a sacramental
   understanding;
g) the significant presentation of the threefold ministry of bishops,
   presbyters and deacons even if they are considered rather as functional
   tasks that can exist concretely in different patterns (22);
h) the responsibility of the ministry is adequately described as "proclaiming and teaching the word of God, celebrating the sacraments
   and guiding the life of the community in its worship, its mission and
   its caring ministry" (13);
i) the statement is more than a theological exposition; it also has a
   pastoral perspective that can both inspire ministers in the exercise of
   their ministry, and help the community to accept them as "heralds and
   ambassadors of Jesus Christ" (11).

We appreciate the fact that ordained ministry is not treated in isolation
but rather in its wider ecclesiological context, in its relationship to the
church as God's people, to its unity, apostolicity and catholicity and its
existence as a local community. But further reflection on ecclesiology
will be needed in the Commission on Faith and Order, in order to put the
ordained ministry in clear perspective. As an illustration, one essential
dimension of the church that remains obscure, although it is of the
greatest importance for understanding and valuing the authority of
ordained ministry, is the sacramental aspect of the whole church, at work
in a particular way in the ministry, in its teaching office, in the administration of the sacraments and in its governing. In a real and effective sense
the church is an icon of the presence of God and his kingdom in the
world. This is always because of God's actual and constant faithfulness to
his promise in Jesus Christ. The basic ministerial structures participate in
that sacramental dimension. Further ecumenical dialogue will have to
deal more fully with that spiritual and sacramental dimension of the
church and its ministry.

Authority of tradition

The text uses the sacred scriptures and especially the New Testament as a basis for its argumentation, showing the uniqueness of Christ's authority, the particular role of the apostles and the spirit in which the ministry must be exercised.

In stating that the church has never been without persons holding specific authority and responsibility (9), the text could not ignore the difficulties that arise in trying to retrace the origin of the actual pattern in the Bible (cf. Comm. 17, Nos 19,22, Comm. 40) and had to try to avoid historic fundamentalism.

The text necessarily had to deal with historic evolution of ministry in the early church, for example, the evolution of the forms of the ordained ministry (19-21), the succession of the apostolic ministry (35-36, and Comm. 36) and the understanding of priesthood. Frequently it gives special weight to an argument from antiquity.[10] One aim of this approach is to contribute to helping communities which have not retained the episcopate to appreciate the episcopate as a sign of the continuity and unity of the church (38) and maybe to recover the sign (53b). Later developments regarding structures, taking place at some points of crisis in history, do not seem to have the same weight in the document as those of the first centuries (19,22). These references to the apostolic times and the first centuries of Christianity are due not only to historic and critical honesty, but have a clear theological weight. That evolution is related to the guidance of the Holy Spirit (19).

The attention given to origins and "antiquity" certainly meets a concern of many churches. But this approach in the document still remains incomplete because too often it involves only a statement of fact and is insufficiently supported by theological reflection on the normativity of such antiquity. In other words, it must be completed by considering also the role of the decisive authority in the discernment of such developments in the past, as well as in regard to the present needs of the church and the ecumenical situation today.

---

[10] "The ministry of... persons (responsible for showing the Church's dependence on Jesus Christ) who *since very early times* have been ordained..." (8); "the Church has *never been without* persons holding specific authority and responsibility" (9); "...*from the beginning*, there were differentiated roles in the community" (9); "The basic reality of an ordained ministry *was present from the beginning*" (Comm. 11); "*Historically*... the threefold ministry *became* the generally accepted pattern in the Church of the *early centuries*"; "Under the particular *historical* circumstances of the *growing* church in the *early centuries*, the succession of bishops became one of the ways... in which the apostolic tradition ...was expressed" (36).

2. PARTICULAR COMMENTS

The calling of the whole people of God

In the line of many texts that have emerged from bilateral dialogues, but also of the *Dogmatic Constitution on the Church* of the Second Vatican Council, it is good to see that the text looks at the problem of the ordained ministry from a broader angle. It starts with a brief theological and ecclesiological reflection upon the calling of the whole people of God. It shows how this calling must be envisioned in the perspective of God's Trinitarian concern for humanity as a whole: the calling of God, the mediation of Jesus Christ and the liberating and renewing power of the Holy Spirit. It is in this light that the document describes some features of the calling of the church, expressing especially its mission to witness and service. As part of this calling, the Holy Spirit bestows on the community diverse and complementary gifts (5) and charisms that form the background of all ministries in the church. We agree with the general understanding of the calling of the people of God, as it is stated in the first section.

The question, "how, according to the will of God and under the guidance of the Holy Spirit, is the life of the Church to be understood and ordered, so that the Gospel may be spread and the community built up in love" (6), is a fair question. The reference to the will of God and the guidance of the Holy Spirit rightly indicates the awareness that church order, at least in its fundamental constitution, is not the result of historical developments and human-made organization. But the question cannot be answered conclusively as long as the questions of who will decide, who will discern God's will in various developments and with what authority, are left open. We believe in fact that certain people are commissioned in the church with a God-given authority to exercise such ministry of decision. Therefore, the question of authority in the church must be studied in relationship to ministry.

The church and the ordained ministry

One of the means by which the church is ordered according to the will of God and under the guidance of the Holy Spirit is through the existence of an ordained ministry. In the description of the chief responsibility of the ordained ministry, given in 13, we recognize the framework of a Catholic understanding of the mission of the ordained ministry. We approve of the way this ministry is already related to the mission of the Twelve. We would suggest that this mission should be related further with Christ's own mission by the Father: "As the Father sent me, so I am sending you" (John 20:21).

We are glad to see that the document mentions the two complementary forms of "representation" of ordained ministers: the representation of the people of God and the representation of Jesus Christ, as heralds, ambassadors, leaders, teachers, pastors (11). In the commentary to 13, when the specificity of the ordained ministry with regard to the participation of the community in fulfilling these functions is mentioned, it declares that "the ordained ministry fulfills these functions in a representative way, providing the focus for the unity of the life and witness of the community" (Comm. 13). The concept of "representation" is a valuable concept which roots in the theological understanding of the churches. But it needs further qualification in the context of the agreed statement, so that through its relation to the Archetypos Christ, the ordained ministry is in and for the church an effective and sacramental reality, by which a minister acts "in persona Christi". This view should also help to explain more fully why, according to the Catholic faith, the eucharist must be presided over by an ordained minister, who represents Christ in a personal and sacramental way (14). In this way, too, the image of the ordained ministry as "focus of its unity" (8, Comm. 13 and 14, in relation to the eucharist) could be deepened. By stressing this sacramental aspect that marks a person before God and the community, we do not want to separate the minister from the community or exalt him above it, because we fully agree with the strong connection the document makes between the ordained ministry and the community (cf. 12). Still, there is a special role for the ordained ministry. We should not hesitate to see, in light of tradition, something of Christ's real and sacramental presence in the ordained minister: a particular sign among others.

The section on "ordained ministry and authority" contains two fine paragraphs on the manner and the spirit in which ordained ministers must exercise their authority with the cooperation of the whole community, focusing on the model of Christ himself and the way he revealed God's authority to the world (16). We agree with these paragraphs. But at the same time the task remains of reflecting upon the ecclesiological dimension and the peculiar nature of this authority. It is rooted, as the document aptly states, in agreement with the Tradition of the church, on the relation between ordination and function, in Jesus Christ "who has received it from the Father and who confers it by the Holy Spirit through the act of ordination" (15).

In considering "ordained ministry and priesthood", the commentary to 17 rightly points to the different applications of the word "priest" and "priesthood" in the New Testament and the church, thus avoiding a confusion of Christ's unique priesthood, the royal and prophetic priesthood of all baptized and the priesthood of certain ordained ministers: they belong to different evolutions in the use of the word "priesthood/priest". In this way it points at the same time to the analogy and the essential difference between them.

This is important, but perhaps needs to be further clarified. In the teaching of the Catholic Church, although the common priesthood of the faithful and the ministerial or hierarchical priesthood are inter-related, each being in its own way a participation in the one priesthood of Christ, they differ from one another in essence and not only in degree.[11] We believe that further study must be done by Faith and Order on this point. We note for example in 17 that in the appropriate reasons for "calling the minister 'priest'", the reality of "sacrifice", mentioned explicitly for Christ and the priesthood of the baptized, is absent, although it belongs inherently to the concept of ordained priesthood. Certain ministers are called priests because of their specific part in presiding at the celebration of the eucharist, as "heralds and ambassadors" of Christ, who gives himself as sacrifice for all. The reference to the eucharist that is made in the commentary to 17 could have been made correctly in the paragraph itself.

We approve of the nuanced way in which the "ministry of men and women in the Church" is treated (II.D). We recognize fully that the experience of the churches which practise the ordination of women constitutes inevitably a challenge to our own position. At the same time we believe that there are theological issues rooted not only in the understanding of Tradition, but also of the scriptures, concerning Christology, which lie at the heart of our convictions and understanding with regard to the admission of women to the ordained ministry (Comm. 18). On this latter point, the text states (18) that "many churches hold that the tradition of the Church in this regard must not be changed". In our view, it would be more accurate to say that we have no authority to change it, since we believe it belongs to the apostolic Tradition of the church. Perhaps this nuance also points to a different conception of apostolic tradition in the BEM text than Catholics would find acceptable. Even if differences on these issues can raise obstacles to recognition of certain ministries, they should never become prejudicial to further reflection upon the ordained ministry within the ecumenical context. "Openness to each other holds the possibility that the Spirit may well speak to one church through the insights of another" (54).

---

[11] Cf. *Lumen Gentium*, 10.

The forms of the ordained ministry

It is important for the future of the ecumenical movement that the text, after having fully recognized the historic evolution of the ministerial pattern in the church, could so explicitly agree on the singular significance of the threefold ministry of bishop, presbyter and deacon, as "the generally accepted pattern in the Church of the early centuries" and as being "still retained today by many churches" (22).

This evolution in the church is seen as more than merely a result of fortuitous events. It is seen in connection with the guidance of the Spirit (19 and 22). And we surely agree with the hope expressed that "the threefold ministry... may serve today as an expression of the unity we seek and also as a means for achieving it" (22). This statement fits within the framework of the church's faith and order through the ages. But it should be ecclesiologically deepened by examining whether the text means that such ministry belongs only to the ecumenical wellbeing (bene esse) of the church, or rather to its constitutive being, rooted in God's will for the church as it has been discerned by the authority in the church. Therefore one has to distinguish between the fundamental and constitutive core of the threefold ministry, as the institutional expression of what was involved in the message of the New Testament, and the historic form, style and organization it has inevitably assumed and will also assume in the future. An ecumenical discernment is needed to see what belongs to the constitutive structure of the church and what to the contingent social organization. The invitation to reform many formal aspects of the threefold pattern (24) in openness to each other and to contextual needs should be taken up.

The description of guiding principles for the exercise of the ordained ministry (26-27), of the functions of the bishops, presbyters and deacons (28-31) and of the variety of charisms (32-33) bring together various elements that are retraceable in various developments and in the historical evolution of the church, in which one recognizes the practice of the church through the ages.

Episcopacy is rightly described as "a focus of unity" (20), as necessary to express and safeguard the unity of the body (23) and as a service of unity at a regional level (27) as "representative pastoral ministers of oversight, continuity and unity in the Church". Even if the text acknowledges the fact that "they relate the Christian community in their area to the wider Church and the universal Church to their community", the description hardly mentions the very traditional and essential collegial aspect of episcopacy. In a unique way, in comparison to other ordained ministers, bishops represent and symbolize in their person their local church and relate it, in communion with the other churches, to the universal church. The ecumenical council becomes thus a representative image of the universal church, because it is a meeting of the college of bishops around the bishop of Rome who, according to the Catholic Church, is the head of this college. While all of this is important, we miss here the clear expression of the teaching function of the bishops, the magisterium, which is a significant aspect that must also be taken into account here, and in the future work of Faith and Order.

We understand that it may not be the purpose, at present, of the Faith and Order Commission to reflect upon the personal expression of a "focus of unity" in the universal church, but one can ask whether that would not be a logical result of the reflections started upon a representative service of oversight, continuity and unity in the church.

Succession in the apostolic tradition

In the context of the divergent practices among the churches, the document deals with the relation between the apostolicity of the church and the apostolic tradition on one side, and the orderly transmission of the ordained ministry (35) and, more especially, the episcopal succession as one of its forms (36), on the other. By doing so it gives the problem a wider ecclesiological relevancy and brings a mutual comprehension for practices, which may seem unacceptable when isolated.

The connection of the apostolic succession with the apostolic tradition, understood as "the continuity in the permanent characteristics of the Church of the apostles", in their witness, proclamation, celebration, service etc. (34), is legitimate. One may even say as in 36: "... the succession of bishops became one of the ways, together with the transmission of the Gospel and the life of the community, in which the apostolic tradition of the Church was expressed". But is there not the tendency here to be content with a listing and a juxtaposition of items which all have to do with the apostolic tradition without showing sufficiently how they have their own function within the totality and how they are related among themselves?

According to the statement, the episcopal succession was understood in the early centuries "as serving, symbolizing and guarding the continuity of the apostolic faith and communion" (36, with reference to Clement of Rome and Ignatius of Antioch in the commentary). And today, even churches which have not retained the episcopate are able to appreciate the episcopal succession "as a sign, though not a guarantee, of the continuity and unity of the church" (38). It is said that there is willingness expressed among them "to accept episcopal succession as a sign of the apostolicity of the life of the whole Church" (38). The text speaks further on of "a need to recover the sign of the episcopal succession" that will strengthen and deepen that continuity with the church of the apostles (53b).

We agree that the "episcopal succession" is of the order of the sign that can signify, through the image of historic transmission, the fact that the church is rooted in the apostolic church around Christ and therefore shows its fundamental apostolicity. However, the meaning of "sign/expression" needs to be clear. In the previous version, *One Baptism, One Eucharist and a Mutually Recognized Ministry* (34), the text spoke of an "effective sign". This indicates better the unique importance of the episcopal succession for the edification of the church through the ages. This is immediately related to the meaning which the ministry of the bishop has in a Catholic ecclesiology: it is more than a function of oversight next to other functions and ministries. In his very personal ministry, the bishop represents the local church entrusted to him. He is its qualified spokesperson in the communion of the churches. At the same time he is the first representative of Jesus Christ in the community. By his ordination to the episcopacy he is commissioned to exercise leadership in the community, to teach with authority and to judge. All other ministries are linked to his and function in relationship to it. Thus his ministry is a sacramental sign of integration and a focus of communion. Through the episcopal succession, the bishop embodies and actualizes both catholicity in time, i.e., the continuity of the church across the generations, as well as the communion lived in each generation. The actual community is thus linked up through a personal sign with the apostolic origins, its teaching and way of living.

In that perspective, episcopal succession can rightly be called a *guarantee* (cf. 38) of the continuity and unity of the church, if one recognizes in it the expression of Christ's faithfulness to the church to the end of time. At the same time it lays upon each individual office-bearer the responsibility to be a faithful and diligent guarantor.

Ordination

When stating that "the Church ordains certain of its members for the ministry in the name of Christ by the invocation of the Spirit and laying on of hands" (39; also 7c, 41, 52), the text describes the act of ordination in a way consonant with the faith and the practice of the Catholic Church. The document specifies three essential dimensions of the ordination: (1) it is "an invocation to God that the new minister be given the power of the Holy Spirit..." (42); (2) it is "a sign of the granting of this prayer by the Lord who gives the gift of the ordained ministry" (43); and (3) it is "an acknowledgement by the Church of the Spirit in the one ordained, and a commitment by both the Church and the ordinand to the new relationship" (44).

This positive evaluation meets in many ways the Catholic concept of ordination as a sacrament: the reality granted is the power of the Holy Spirit (42); the ordained ministry as a gift given by the Lord; a sign signifying a spiritual relationship (43) for "a new relation which is established between this minister and the local Christian community" (42,44). And this is acknowledged and given in a sign, the act of ordination (42). "Ordination is a sign performed in faith that the spiritual relationship signified is present in, with and through the words spoken, the gestures made and the forms employed" (43). In a quite comprehensive sense, in which historical and spiritual references are made, the institution of the act of ordination is related "with Jesus Christ and the apostolic witness" (39). "The laying on of hands is the sign of the gift of the Spirit, rendering visible the fact that the ministry was instituted in the revelation accomplished in Christ, and reminding the Church to look to him as the source of its commission" (39). While this seems to be implied in the passages just cited, Catholics would like it to be stated clearly that ordination is not only a sign, but an effective sign.

In the description of ordination essential elements for the sacrament are enumerated, without however calling it a sacrament. Using the word twice in a wider, but significant way, once as an adjective (41) and once as an adverb (43), it points in the direction of a sacramental understanding. Among the churches and communities represented in Faith and Order, ordination is described as a sacrament by some, but not by others. This perhaps explains why the word is not used. At the same time, in the line of the faith, the essentials of a sacramental understanding can be recognized in the broad treatment given to it in this text.

Furthermore, we mention in passing three elements that take up Catholic concerns: (1) the specifying intention in ordination (39), (2) the eucharistic context of ordination (41), and (3) the statement that ordination is never repeated in recognition of the God-given charism of ministry. All of this points to an important convergence on ordination achieved in BEM. But one that still does not express clearly the Catholic conviction that ordination is indeed a sacrament.

One point is not treated in a way that is sufficient according to the Catholic faith, namely the problem of the competent minister of ordination. This is important because, in fact, it is through the *epiklesis* prayed for by the competent minister that the gift of the Spirit is conferred on the person ordained (cf. 43). We understand the difficulty arising in a statement expressing the views of churches and ecclesial communities which differ on the qualified minister. We appreciate the statement that even churches which have not retained the episcopate want to express the continuity in apostolic faith, worship and mission in the fact that "ordination is always done... by persons in whom the Church recognizes the authority to transmit the ministerial commission" (37).

Our view, however, is that ordination is a sacrament. The competent minister of this sacrament is a bishop who stands in the authentic apostolic succession and who acts in the person of Christ. We therefore ask the Commission on Faith and Order to reflect on the ecclesiological meaning of the episcopal succession for ordination. We believe that its necessity is due to the fact that the episcopal succession signifies and actualizes the sacramental link of the ministry — first of all of the episcopal ministry itself — with the apostolic origin. It is rooted in the sacramental nature of the church. It is only when the question of the minister of the ordination is settled adequately that a serious step towards recognition of ministry will become possible.

Towards the mutual recognition of the ordained ministries

The unsatisfactory way in which "Baptism, Eucharist and Ministry" deals with the problem of the mutual recognition of the ordained ministry shows that we touch here upon a crux in the endeavours towards Christian unity. At the heart of it stands the very concrete issue of sacramental ordination related to this issue of the historic episcopal succession. Many particular questions however cannot be solved before entering in concrete union negotiations. One way forward seems to lie in increasing mutual respect by the churches and ecclesial communities for each other.

We can acknowledge the many ways in which continuity in apostolic faith, worship and mission has been preserved in communities which have not retained the form of historic episcopate. As the Second Vatican Council says: "The Christian way of life of these brethren is nourished by faith in Christ. It is strengthened by the grace of baptism and the hearing of the word of God. This way of life expresses itself in private prayer, in meditation on the scriptures, in the life of a Christian family, and in the worship of the community gathered together to praise God" (*UR* 23; cf. *LG* 15). But we believe that ordained ministry requires sacramental ordination by a bishop standing in the apostolic succession. We hope that a growing fraternal solidarity of collaboration, common reflection, prayer and service between churches and ecclesial communities, and particularly their ministries, can reach a point of seeing whether, or in what terms, an ordained ministry recognized by all might become possible.

Meanwhile we suggest again that the theological reflection upon the meaning of the episcopal succession for the understanding of the church and its ministry should be deepened. It will not be an opportunistic "recovering of the sign of episcopal succession" that will solve the problem, but newly gained convictions about God's will and the guidance of the Holy Spirit regarding the constitutive features of church order, the episcopal succession and its exercise in ordination.

It must be clear that the recognition of ordained ministry cannot be isolated from its ecclesiological context. The recognition of the ordained ministry and of the ecclesial character of a Christian community are indissolubly and mutually related. To the extent that it can be recognized that communion now exists between churches and ecclesial communities, however imperfect that communion may be, there is implied some recognition of the ecclesial reality of the other. The question that follows is what does this communion imply for the way we perceive the ministry of the other? This perhaps is one question that should be taken up when attention is given to the fundamental ecclesiological dimension of the problem of recognition of the ordained ministry.

Since, in our view, ordained ministry requires sacramental ordination in the apostolic succession, it is premature to make pronouncements upon the form a public act of mutual recognition of churches and their ministries would have (55). Rather it is necessary now to work towards unity in faith on this central ecclesiological issue.

IV. CONSEQUENCES OF BEM
FOR ECUMENICAL RELATIONS AND DIALOGUE

1. Consequences concerning ecumenism in general
The BEM text makes some valuable suggestions on ecumenical relations in general.

A holistic approach to ecumenism
One suggestion it makes is that our approach to ecumenism must be holistic. BEM suggests this in several ways. First, the four areas of inquiry asked of the churches by Faith and Order in relationship to BEM encourage the churches to reflect on the inter-relationship of the different aspects of the ecumenical movement. Theological dialogue must not be isolated from other ecumenical efforts to break down barriers between Christians. Rather, each aspect of ecumenism must nourish and be nourished by others. Therefore, just as the theological dialogue must

continue, so too must the dialogue of charity that fosters increasing personal contacts on all levels of the church, including the highest levels. These contacts bring understanding. There must also be efforts of common witness between our churches and communities through joint service in matters of evangelization, charity and justice. In this way, we can reach out from beyond the barriers that separate us to forge links that bind us to one another in Christ, in our service to the world.

Secondly, BEM reminds us of the importance of multilateral ecumenical engagement. Both bilateral and multilateral conversations are valuable instruments in the ecumenical movement. In the evolution of the ecumenical documents on baptism, eucharist and ministry, there has been a mutual influence in the treatment of these issues in BEM and in the bilaterals, and a theological and methodological convergence.[12] Furthermore, the multilateral context provides a framework that enables a wide variety of churches and communities to encounter one another on a continuous basis. Some encounter others only within a multilateral framework. When they encounter each other in both, the multilateral framework helps also to ensure that a growing understanding with one partner in a bilateral dialogue will not lead to alienation from others.

The goal of visible unity

Another lesson from or consequence of BEM is that it keeps before Christians this goal of visible unity towards which they must move. It speaks of this goal in the preface. The text of each of the three areas concentrates on those aspects of the theme that relate in some way to problems of mutual recognition leading to unity. Thus the development of the text leads to the need to work for "mutual recognition of baptism" (B15), and towards "unity in eucharistic celebration and communion" (E28), and for "mutual recognition of the ordained ministries" (M51ff.). Though the notion of visible unity still needs to be clarified from an ecumenical point of view, BEM is a reminder to us that the ecumenical movement aims not only at a renewal of attitudes of Christians, but also at a rethinking of relationships between divided Christian communities.

Towards the next step

We believe that BEM is indicative of an important level of convergence on these issues. There are issues needing further development, and some

---

[12] See *Report* to the *Fourth Forum on Bilateral Conversations*, Faith and Order Paper No. 125, Geneva, WCC, 1985.

issues that have not yet been addressed. But what has been achieved, as reflected in BEM, makes us realize the convergence, and the similarities growing even with those who have been furthest from us doctrinally. This in itself is a stimulant for further dialogue towards another step forward on the way to unity in faith, and the visible unity of Christians.

2. Particular consequences stemming from each text

In regard to "Baptism", BEM can help us to reflect again on baptism as a basis for Christian unity. The Catholic Church and every Christian community should deepen its recognition of the real bonds of faith and life in Christ that exist between communities which celebrate baptism authentically and ought to find ways of expressing this recognition. BEM presents important ways of seeing common ground between those communities which practise baptism of infants and those practising baptism of adults only. Although, as we have already noted, the text is not completely satisfactory from our point of view on some issues concerning baptism, it is a major contribution to the ecumenical movement. It is on the basis of baptism that we can say that, despite our continuing divisions, a real, though imperfect communion already exists between divided Christians. The BEM text explains the baptismal basis of this communion that already exists.

In regard to "Eucharist", the reception of the Lima text on eucharist by a church would not have the immediate result of allowing reciprocal eucharistic sharing. This is because the notion of eucharistic sharing for the Catholic Church is intimately related to other basic factors such as unity in the whole faith of the church, and particularly in regard to the church and the ministry.

As already noted, we are not totally satisfied with every aspect of the BEM text on the eucharist. On some serious points it does not say enough to represent the fullness of Christian faith. Still we recognize the significance of the convergence and even areas of agreement on many points of eucharistic thinking that the text represents. Thus we would say that if all the churches and ecclesial communities are able to accept at least the theological understanding and description of the celebration of the eucharist as described in BEM and implement it as part of their normal life, we believe that this would be an important development, and that these divided Christians now stood on a new level in regard to achieving common faith on the eucharist.

Concerning "Ministry", what BEM says is important, although we have pointed to areas where further study is necessary. In regard to recognition of ministry, for us it is not only agreement on the question of apostolic succession, but also being situated within it, that is necessary for recognition of ordination.

But if some of the proposals on ministry in BEM were generally accepted, that would constitute a major step towards Christian unity. For example, if the threefold ministry of bishop, presbyter and deacon, explained in BEM, were adopted generally by Christian communities, that would put the churches and ecclesial communities on a new level of relationship, even if the precise meaning of the threefold ministry would still need further refinement.

BEM notes grounds on which mutual respect for ministries can grow. It states that "in churches which practise the succession through the episcopate, it is increasingly recognized that a continuity in apostolic faith, worship and mission has been preserved in churches which have not retained the form of historic episcopate" (37). It notes however that "these considerations do not diminish the importance of the episcopal ministry" (38) and many of the former "express willingness to accept episcopal succession as a sign of the apostolicity of the life of the whole Church". These considerations remind us of the teachings of the Second Vatican Council which say that "the brethren divided from us also carry out many liturgical actions of the Christian religion. In ways that vary according to the condition of each church, or community, these liturgical actions most certainly can truly engender a life of grace and, one must say, can aptly give access to the communion of salvation." It follows that the separated churches and communities as such "have been by no means deprived of significance and importance in the mystery of salvation" (*UR* 3).

There are already grounds on which mutual respect can begin to grow and dimensions of fellowship between our communities can be built, reflecting the levels of communion that now exist. But this is still inadequate. We need to continue the dialogue for unity of faith in regard to ministry as well as other matters, as we move towards full communion.

V. CONCLUSION

The study of BEM has been for many Catholics an enriching experience. Catholics can find in BEM much that they can agree with. At the same time there are important areas related to baptism, eucharist and ministry clearly in need of further study within the ecumenical context that the Commission on Faith and Order provides. We rejoice in the convergence that has taken place and look to further growth towards unity.

For the Catholic Church, the truths of faith are not divided from one another. They constitute a unique organic whole. Therefore full agreement on the sacraments is related to agreement on the nature of the church. The sacraments, including baptism, receive their full significance and efficacy from the comprehensive ecclesial reality on which they depend and which they manifest. Nor can the goal of the unity of divided Christians be reached without agreement on the nature of the church.

BEM is a significant result and contribution to the ecumenical movement. It demonstrates clearly that serious progress is being made in the quest for visible Christian unity.

With this response, the Catholic Church wants to encourage Faith and Order to continue its valuable work for seeking unity in faith as the basis for visible unity. We recommit ourselves to this process with other churches and ecclesial communities in that serious task to which Christ calls all of us.

SLOVAK EVANGELICAL CHURCH OF THE AUGSBURG CONFESSION IN THE CSSR

1. It is our view that the BEM document is not definitive and has not been worked out in every detail. We welcome its endeavour to distinguish the points of agreement and divergence in the doctrine and life of the churches. This endeavour follows from the aim to make it clear that Christ has only one church on earth. The document has in mind a real convergence or coming together of the churches. This, however, can take place only if there is adherence to the whole truth as we learn it from the word of God. We therefore propose that in solving the problem of what the church is and accomplishes, recourse should be had to the position taken up in the Augsburg Confession, that it is sufficient for a true church if in it the pure gospel is preached and the sacraments are administered as instituted by Jesus Christ. This description is adequate but neither of these two essentials should be missing.

2. In connection with the response prepared by the theologians of those churches in Czechoslovakia which are members of the WCC, and which we basically endorse, we would stress a few principles which remain inadequately expressed in the statement:
1) that the baptism of children has the same validity as that of adults;
2) that the non-repeatable nature of baptism should be held to — in all churches; and
3) that the role of godparents in baptism should be clarified.

As regards the Lord's supper attention must be clearly drawn to the necessity for confession. Confession does not reduce the joyful eucharistic character of the Lord's supper, but is the immediate precondition for it. Repentance in fact shows specially clearly that we have a share in communion with Christ in the Lord's supper despite our sinfulness.

● 300,000 members, 384 parishes, 3 bishops, 350 pastors. This response was adopted by the General Convention of the Church in Bratislava on 7 December 1985.

In the section on the ministry it should be clearly stated that the ministry does not constitute the *esse* of the church but is the church's fitting instrument if it points wholly towards Christ.

3. Answering in order the four questions of BEM (p. x), we offer the following opinion:

a) On the extent to which our church can recognize in the BEM document the faith of the church through the ages: we appreciate the document's attempt to arrive at what over a long period has shown itself to be the content of faith and life in the churches. But here we expect it to be made explicit that baptism is in fact a sacrament, and that communion is efficacious for all communicants although the way it works varies with the way individuals receive it. The emphasis on the invocation of the Holy Spirit in the Lord's supper is valuable but the saving effect of this sacrament derives not from the invocation but solely from the action of the Holy Spirit himself. In the section on the ministry we miss an emphasis on the significance of all those who preach or proclaim the gospel today, not just (as the document defines the ministry) bishops, presbyters and deacons. It is not enough to stop short at the historical description of ministers; it is necessary also to move into the present. A notable feature of the document is, in our view, the effort it makes to define the role of episcopal succession within the apostolic tradition.

b) On the consequences our church can draw from this text for its dialogues with other churches, we wish to indicate that the document will be a stimulus to us for such dialogues as are founded on every aspect of the church's — and the churches' — actual situation. It goes without saying that in this it will not be our intention to deviate from the truth for the sake of compromises.

c) On the guidance our church can take from the document for our worship, educational, ethical and spiritual life: we shall give detailed consideration to all three sections of BEM as regards any sphere of the church's activity in so far as such is mentioned in the document. We seek to be stimulated by the document to deepen the faith and life of the church in every respect.

d) Finally, on the suggestions we can make to the commission that prepared the text: it will be necessary to produce a definitive text of the document, to distinguish properly the essentials from what is less fundamental, and to indicate where there already exists such agreement among the churches as representing movement from convergence towards consensus — a consensus, moreover, that can be formulated in keeping with the doctrines of the faith.

BEM is an extraordinarily important document. This is especially true because until now no discussion concerning all the churches has been conducted over such a wide field since the "ecumenical councils" met more than a thousand years ago and took decisions relating to faith and order. We do not expect any quick results, but by its response our church wishes to make a contribution such that the outcome will in every respect be to the advantage of the church of God.

> Prof. Dr Jan Michalko
> Presiding Bishop (Generalbischof)

EVANGELICAL LUTHERAN CHURCH IN BRUNSWICK (FRG)

a) The Evangelical Lutheran Church in Brunswick gratefully takes note of the convergence text and welcomes the hereby vitalized dialogue for further clarifications and for strengthening the ecumenical community.
b) We declare our willingness to participate in the process of evaluation in order to help overcome divergences.
c) As our response to the four questions which were put in the preface of the convergence text on "Baptism, Eucharist and Ministry", please find enclosed a text which is meant to be a contribution of the Evangelical Lutheran Church in Brunswick to the process of reception.

Baptism

1. Responding to the question: "... the extent to which your church can recognize in this text the faith of the Church through the ages".

Our church thinks highly of the attempt to define the meaning of baptism for the "faith of the Church" by relating to basic New Testament witnesses and by elaborating on the biblical teaching on baptism by hinting at the patristic traditions and the baptismal practice in the old church. We recognize the "faith of the Church", which is in harmony with this elaboration, in numerous basic statements of the convergence text on baptism.

Generally we find ourselves in agreement with the way in which the convergence text defines the relationship between God's gift and man's response. The heritage of the Reformation, however, by which our church lives, demands special importance to be attached to infant baptism as an expression of God's undeserved grace by which we are born again.

● 540,000 members, 13 dioceses, 397 congregations, 278 pastors.

Therefore it is desirable to come up with a clearer definition of baptism as a gift and human response as a consequence. In defining the relationship between baptism and faith in the various baptismal practices our church suggests to replace the term "baptism of believers" by "baptism of adults". The term "corporate faith" is to be rejected if it is acceptable if it is meant to stress the necessity of embodying a child into the community of believers as part of the practice of infant baptism.

The text has a strong tendency of tying faith to sanctification. Out of the tradition of our church we understand faith as trusting in God's promise out of which trust new life emerges through sanctification.

In our church, too, there is an ongoing discussion about the relationship between baptism and confirmation. Often the fundamental importance of baptism is not made clear properly. If the text is based on the presupposition that baptism once and for all is the beginning of participation in Jesus Christ and is valid for the whole life of the baptized, we agree. This is where our dialogue about confirmation has to start from. The symbolic additions and interpretations of baptismal practices as they are described under Nos 18 and 19 must be rejected in those cases where they stand in the way of the central meaning of baptism.

2. Responding to the question: "... the consequences your church can draw from this text for its relations and dialogues with other churches, particularly with those churches which also recognize the text as an expression of the apostolic faith".

In accordance with the convergence text our church considers the common baptism which ties us to Christ in faith to be the basic bond of unity. On the basis of agreement about the meaning of baptism and a mutual recognition of baptismal practice we express our readiness to take further steps on the way towards a strengthening of a common understanding of baptism; about this readiness we will inform those churches which, like ours, recognize baptism as an expression of apostolic faith.

As a church which baptizes both infants and adults we cannot but expect from churches which baptize adults only that they may recognize our baptismal practice as a Christian practice. Furthermore it is and will be our position that the distinction between "baptism of infants" and "baptism of believers" is a problematic one. Our understanding of baptism does not allow such a polarization. The experiences made with conducting child baptism and adult baptism should be incorporated into the ecumenical dialogue. Hereby everything should be avoided that might put into doubt the common conviction of the unrepeatability of baptism. The convergence text does not state clearly how faith and conversion relate to the proclamation of the word. The teaching that baptism (adult baptism) includes confession of sins and conversion of the heart (No. 4) is acceptable only if it includes the assumption that the proclamation of the gospel had reached the baptismal candidate already and that it leads him to conversion and confession of sins. Future discussions about the further development of the convergence text will have to face the task to move from the relationship of baptism and faith to the relationship between baptism, proclamation of the gospel, and faith.

3. Responding to the question: "... the guidance your church can take from this text for its worship, educational, ethical, and spiritual life and witness".

Our church will have to ask itself if its baptismal practice and baptismal understanding are in harmony with the eschatological dynamics as described in the convergence text which says that "it is a sign of the Kingdom of God and of the life of the world to come" (No. 7). For fundamental reasons our church will not change its practice of conducting baptisms as part of public worship services, especially on the main Christian holidays. We will put additional efforts into reminding the church members of their own baptism. The convergence text reminds our church of the great responsibility which it has for the education of the baptized children, to lead them towards their own consciousness of belonging to Christ (No. 16).

4. Responding to the question: "... the suggestion your church can make for the ongoing work of Faith and Order as it relates the material of this text on baptism, eucharist and ministry to the long-range research project 'Towards the Common Expression of the Apostolic Faith Today'".

Our church suggests that holy scripture should again and more strongly be considered the foundation of theology and church and that through the help of holy scripture the Trinitarian teaching and practice of baptism should become more profound and more lively (*norma normans*).

Eucharist

1. Responding to the question: "... the extent to which your church can recognize in this text the faith of the Church through the ages".

Our church appreciates the attempt of the convergence text to describe fundamental aspects of the "apostolic faith" and the "faith of the Church through the ages" and thus to give expression to the richness and fullness of the eucharist. We welcome the stressing of the central position which the eucharist occupies in the life and faith of the church. Moreover we welcome the attempt to stress the joyful character of the eucharist.

We think, however, that the mystery of the real presence of Christ in the bread and wine of the eucharist should be stated more clearly. We miss the use of the term "holy communion" instead of "eucharist" and the authoritativeness of the institution of holy communion by the Lord — as is indicated in the headline of chapter I. Then we feel that the rootedness of the joyful character of the eucharist in penitence and forgiveness, which is part of receiving the eucharist, is not elaborated on clearly enough. We are of the opinion that the eschatological and sacramental character of the eucharist recedes too much. It is this very characteristic which is in accordance with "the faith of the Church through the ages".

2. Responding to the question: "... the consequences your church can draw from this text for its relations and dialogues with other churches, particularly with those churches which also recognize the text as an expression of the apostolic faith".

The convergence texts offer starting points in interchurch dialogues, including dialogues between and in local congregations. In such dialogues the recognition of convergence must not exclude the search for consensus in the one truth of apostolic faith in relation to the eucharistic gifts. Our church grants eucharistic hospitality to those who believe in Jesus Christ, the one who instituted the holy supper, as being present under bread and wine.

3. Responding to the question: "... the guidance your church can take from this text for its worship, educational, ethical, and spiritual life and witness".

For the life of our church the convergence text gives useful directions in stressing that the eucharist, by being celebrated oftentimes, should regain the importance which it deserves. The *epiklesis* as part of the eucharist can be considered an enrichment as long as the works of the Holy Spirit are not seen as being separate from the works of the word of God. The suggestions how to treat the eucharistic elements properly can be considered a help to celebrate the eucharist according to apostolic usage. For us it is important that the Christians' responsibility towards the world is rooted in and stems from holy communion.

4. Responding to the question: "... the suggestions your church can make for the ongoing work of Faith and Order as it relates the material of this text on Baptism, Eucharist and Ministry to its long-range research project 'Towards the Common Expression of the Apostolic Faith Today'".

In the future work of the Commission the churches involved should clarify if and to what degree the term "apostolic faith" really provides a common basis. Agreement in this respect would lead to a more profound understanding of the eucharist. The term "faith of the Church through the ages" presupposes a certain understanding of tradition which needs further clarification. Moreover the question should be raised if and to what degree certain liturgical traditions of the various churches are of importance beyond the "apostolic faith" or alongside it. According to the Lutheran confession (Confessio Augustana VII) agreement in "apostolic faith" (word and sacrament) suffices. In that the goal of eucharistic unity has not been reached yet other forms of church unity should move the churches closer to each other.

Ministry

1. Responding to the question: "... the extent to which your church can recognize in this text the faith of the Church through the ages".

The church as a whole is called into the ministry of reconciliation. This ministry is apostolic because it is derived from the apostolic witness. Thus a possibility arises to understand succession as succession in proclamation of the gospel and in teaching. "The Church is apostolic if it remains faithful to the faith and the mission of the Apostles" (Uppsala 1968). The Lima document reminds us of the plurality of ministries in the New Testament. It reminds us, too, that the church needs a ministry of vigilance so that the teachings and the unity of the church may be safeguarded. Our church can identify itself to a great degree with the statements made on the meaning, the act and the conditions of ordination.

2. Responding to the question: "... the consequences your church can draw from this text for its relations and dialogues with other churches, particularly with those churches which also recognize the text as an expression of the apostolic faith".

Some churches of the catholic wing (Anglican, Orthodox, Roman Catholic) hold fast to the position that the episcopal system which developed through the first few centuries after Christ was wrought by the Spirit and is therefore an integral part of the church. We expect our understanding of the ministry not to be considered heretic. For the churches of the Reformation, too, the order of the church is not a matter of unimportance. We have reservations, though, when it comes to copying the threefold pattern of ministry as it emerged in some churches.

3. Responding to the question: "... the guidance your church can take from this text for its worship, educational, ethical, and spiritual life and witness".

Very helpful for us is the repeated stress which the text lays upon our responsibility for the unity of the church and the necessity to remain faithful to the faith and the mission of the apostles. The church cannot be built according to the needs of individuals or individual groups; it lives by the continuity of Christ's own mission. We find it helpful, too, that the text hints at the importance of an orderly passing on of the apostolic faith.

4. Responding to the question: "... the suggestions your church can make for the ongoing work of Faith and Order as it relates the material of this text on baptism, eucharist and ministry to its long-range research project 'Towards the Common Expression of the Apostolic Faith To-day'".

The work on the long-range research project should include the challenges which modern society with its fast developments and changes poses to the church. The churches differ in their views and understanding of women's ordination. The understanding of women's ordination as well as the issue of the ministry of men and women in the church should be dealt with furthermore. The questions of succession through the office of the bishop, succession through proclamation of the gospel and teaching of the church, and mutual recognition of ministries require further work. Then, further work should be conducted in relation to the question if and how "God, being faithful to his promise in Christ, enters sacramentally into contingent, historical forms of human relationship and uses them for his purpose" (No. 43b).

Unanimously adopted
Synod, May 1985

INDEPENDENT EVANGELICAL LUTHERAN CHURCH (FEDERAL REPUBLIC OF GERMANY AND WEST BERLIN)

I. Defining the position

It is not to be expected that the statements of the Lima document on baptism, the Lord's supper and ministry, on which representatives of so many Christian churches were at work, will be determined by or expressed in the language and tradition of the Lutheran Church. If one is to do justice to the text, one must be open to new insights, forms of expression, and material which are not to be found in the Lutheran confessional writings. This is obvious, and need not in any way be seen as a surrendering of one's own confession. For the Lutheran confession itself demands that it be tested by the standard of holy scripture, and it is definitely open to enrichments.

On the other hand, one must also be aware of what cannot be given up by Lutheran churches, not only because it is one with their confessions, but even more so because it is simply demanded by the witness of scripture.

The positions which must be preserved unconditionally are the following:

1. Holy scripture is normative for the understanding of baptism, the Lord's supper, and ministry, and it determines their content and nature.
2. The soteriological objective of these gifts of Christ to his church dare not be obscured.
3. The character of baptism, eucharist and ministry as institutions and gifts of Christ must be clearly emphasized. Baptism and eucharist are gifts of God from above (*katabatische Richtung*), which call the church to receive them in faith, from which faith arise thanksgiving and praise.

● 37,000 members, 140 parishes.

4. The fundamental axiom that the Spirit of God is bound to the means of grace is to be given its due validity.

5. Confession must be given to the effective power of the words of Christ, which makes the water in baptism a "washing of regeneration", and which creates the real presence of the body and blood of Christ in the elements of the eucharist.

II. On the preface and the use of scripture

The preface gives information concerning the history of the Lima document. Fundamental assertions concerning the understanding of the whole are woven into this description.

1. The Lima document is to make clear "the remarkable degree of agreement" which has been attained among the churches of the World Council of Churches.

This agreement is not described as a "consensus". But the "churches have begun to discover many promising convergences in their shared convictions and perspectives". In their understanding of the faith, the churches have much in common, even though theological forms of expression are different (ix).

2. The aim is full consensus among the churches, which the Lima document itself is to help in bringing about.

This consensus is understood as "that experience of life and articulation of faith necessary to realize and maintain the church's visible unity". It is a gift of the Spirit and it is "realized as a communal experience before it can be articulated by common efforts in words" (ix).

3. The Lima document does not intend to be a comprehensive theological presentation on baptism, eucharist, and ministry, nor can it be that.

Rather "the agreed text purposely concentrates on those aspects of the theme that have been directly or indirectly related to the problems of mutual recognition leading to unity". Accordingly, we are concerned with "the major areas of the theological convergence" (ix).

The conclusions as to the self-understanding of the Lima document arising from these clues are the following:

1. The Lima document is a stage on the way of the churches to the announcement of full consensus and the visible unity of the church.

2. This way is determined by the experience of life and articulation of faith as they can be comprehended in descriptions of convergence. With his gifts the Spirit of God brings about the visible unity of the church through the experience of life and the articulation of faith.

3. The decisive question will be in what way the gospel and scripture have been made use of in the Lima document and its view of faith.

Concerning the use of scripture, the following observations can be directed as a question to Lima:

1. The "Tradition of the Gospel testified in Scripture, transmitted in and by the Church through the power of the Holy Spirit", is the point of reference for the theological argumentation (ix).

Does this mean that the tradition of the gospel in the church, i.e., the history of the passing on of the gospel in the church, has its own importance parallel to the gospel itself as it is testified to in scripture?

2. In point of fact, the statements concerning baptism, the eucharist, and the ministry are derived first of all from the experience of life and articulation of the faith of the churches.

Scripture speaks only as witness of the fact that the gospel has been passed on in baptism, the eucharist, and the ministry; it does not speak as the basis for the gospel.

Is scripture still seen as the witness to the source of the gospel? And is its word still recognized to be absolutely fundamental and determinative?

3. The text of scripture is often understood and interpreted from the experience of life and the articulation of faith in the churches.

For example, the eucharist seems to be a challenge to offer resistance to the injustices of the world (§ 20). Again, the biblical expression "Kingdom of God" is described as an embodiment of the present-day expectation of peace (§§ 22-26). Both of these things take place without consideration of the actual sense (of the scripture) gained by attention to philology and history. Do we see here a use of scripture which allows socio-cultural relations to obscure and pervert the point of scripture, i.e., the saving action of God in Jesus Christ?

4. The simple wording of scripture does not get its due, for the comforting address in the gospel — think only of Luther's use of the "for you" in the Small Catechism — becomes an appeal to conduct in accordance with the gospel.

Is it, accordingly, still possible to recognize God as the one who acts and works in the gospel? Is scripture in Lima perverted finally to law?

These questions are put to Lima from the understanding of the gospel that has been granted us in the Reformation of Luther. We want to see this understanding given consideration in the ecumenical dialogue, and we ourselves cannot give it up in any circumstances.

III. Concerning baptism

1. The statement of convergence here makes use of many biblical texts — something to be welcomed. Yet it must be remarked that the biblical

statements concerning baptism are not really the norm nor the determining content of the document. The institution of baptism is linked to the Tradition of the church rather than to the command of the risen Lord; and the liturgy of the church is used as much as holy scriptures to unfold the meaning of the baptismal sentences; no difference in principle is made between the one and the other authority. More important still is that the total content of the statement gains a twilight-like uncertainty which no longer guarantees that clear biblical statements are characterized as "images" in contrast with one reality; there is continual reference to the determinative contextual relevancy to the modern day — all with the use of classical terminology; so, we find regular use of the concepts of liberation theology (see the preface: "Hence, although the language of the text is largely classical in reconciling historical controversies, the driving force is frequently contextual and contemporary").

2. Many formulations of the Lima document, e.g. baptism as "incorporation into Christ" (§1), as "cleansing of the heart of all sin" (§4), presuppose that God is at work in baptism. Still, there is no really clear witness to baptism as a saving means of grace. For, in the first place, these statements are made of those who are already Christians and saved people. So, there is no place where baptism is declared to work faith as the washing of regeneration. Secondly, baptism is so defined as to include the thought that it is an action of man, i.e., of the one being baptized. In the process, the relation between the divine and the human action is not satisfactorily clarified, nor is it shown whether there is any power in baptism if this human action is lacking. And thirdly, it remains an open question whether the gift of the Holy Spirit takes place through baptism itself or through additional actions, or even directly and immediately. All this means a relativizing of the connection between baptism as the washing of water in the word and the Holy Spirit, and it leads to speaking of baptism in "its full significance", to which it is obviously necessary to contrast baptism in its incomplete significance. On the other hand, one must ask whether a kind of indelible mark is declared to be the effect of baptism — a non-biblical idea — when it is asserted that "God implants in their hearts the first instalment of their inheritance as sons and daughters of God".

3. Again, it is to be welcomed that the baptismal statement pays special attention to the relation of baptism and faith, and emphasizes both the necessity of faith for the reception of the salvation imparted in baptism and the fruit of baptism for the life of Christians. However, it is not asserted that God according to his good pleasure works faith through baptism as the washing of regeneration and so also accepts infants into his

kingdom. Nor is faith characterized, in a way not to be misunderstood, as trusting reception of salvation and not as a work of man (commitment!). In accordance with the criticism is the fact that an endeavour is made to put on the same level infant baptism and believers' baptism (as if infant baptism takes place without faith!), a presenting and blessing of children in a service preceding the latter. This factual equality of infant baptism with a substitute act which has neither been instituted by Christ nor provided with a special promise is not acceptable. It empties baptism of all content, and gives the presenting and blessing of infants a dignity which it can never possess.

4. In the convergent declaration, baptism as gift and action of God and as action of man at the same time are so interwoven that a clear distinction between justification and sanctification appears to be no longer possible. Without a clear statement concerning the position of baptism in the distinction between law and gospel, it is not possible to teach rightly about it, just as one cannot do that without appropriate statements concerning sin. In both respects the statements are completely unsatisfactory.

5. In spite of all the praiseworthy struggle to work for the reciprocal recognition by the churches of the baptism carried out by them, the convergent statement suffers from its failure to point out the decisive, biblical criteria for a valid baptism, criteria that cannot be surrendered, in contrast to actions that are not necessary.

6. Reciprocally-recognized baptism is rightly picked out as a sign of unity. But it is embodied in an understanding of church and bound up with thinking concerning unity which ignores the separation from untruth commanded by the Lord of the church, and which quite without criticism unites what the World Council of Churches does with what the Lord wants.

7. In view of the decisive weaknesses that have been pointed out, we cannot approve the baptismal statement of the Lima document.

IV. Concerning the eucharist

1. It is good to note that in this connection Lima incorporates the understanding of the eucharist in the context of eucharistic practice and piety, and works statements concerning the Lord's supper into the celebration of the eucharist. However, it is not enough to draw attention to roots of the eucharist in the meal celebrations of the earthly Jesus and exalted Lord as testified to in the New Testament. The function of holy scripture as a critical norm also for the understanding of the eucharist and celebration of it also today is neglected.

2. In spite of the assertion "the Church receives the eucharist as a gift from the Lord" (§1), Lima gives excessive weight to the action of the church in its evaluation of *anamnesis* and *epiklesis*. The thanksgiving of the church and its sacrifice of praise always accompany the gift of the Lord, certainly, but they do not in the first place lend reality to the eucharistic occurrence. The concept of sacrifice which has been put as the base of the Lima statement gives encouragement to this misunderstanding that the gift-character of the eucharistic celebration is a secondary matter. With the result that the soteriological goal, the particular importance of the words "given and shed for you for the forgiveness of sins", and the assuring of faith in time of temptation of the forgiveness that comes *extra nos* (outside of us), are obscured.

A concept of sin which is derived from inner-human ways of acting and not from the position of man before God (*coram Deo*) encourages this distortion, as does the regular elimination of the thought of judgment in relation to creation and the world.

3. Even if the church ought not to forget the responsibility given it for the creation and the world in its celebration of the eucharist, nevertheless it is not concerned in the sacrament with bringing about an "ongoing restoration of the world's situation and the human condition" (§20). Neither can it bring itself cooperatively into the once-for-all expiatory sacrifice of Christ; it can only receive what Christ gives it.

4. Lima gives much space to the working of the Holy Spirit in its statements on the eucharist, but it pays no attention to repentance and faith in those who receive the sacrament as the chief result of this working. It rather furthers the misconception that the Spirit, apart from and alongside the words of Christ, brings about the eucharistic presence of the Lord.

5. Instead of the real presence of the body and blood of Christ brought about by the sole activity of the words of the Lord, we have according to Lima a mere personal presence brought about by the Spirit. The proclaimed identity (*praedicatio identica*) of the body and blood with the elements, and the *manducatio impiorum* (i.e., true eating by the unbelieving) that follows from it, seem to have been surrendered.

As a whole, there is a critical lack in Lima on the eucharist in that the matters still in controversy among the churches are covered up. The text is ambiguous in many places. The dominant symbolism of universal salvation threatens to cover up the essentials of the sacrament. Lima does not speak clearly enough about faith which the Spirit brings about, without which the church cannot celebrate the eucharist, and without which Christians cannot receive this sacrament for their salvation. It is rather the case that the sentences speaking of its relation to the world remove attention from its character as gift.

On the positive side, it is to be remarked that Lima understands the eucharist as the centre and the sum of the worship life of the church. In keeping with this, it recommends frequent, at least every Sunday, celebration of the eucharist and encourages frequent reception of the sacrament. In this way, a number of doubtful tendencies leading to an individualizing of the sacrament are averted. In addition, Lima stresses the joyful nature of the eucharistic meal and its eschatological perspective. This is an emphasis that is an especially happy one, even though a series of individual sentences in this connection remain unsatisfactory.

V. Concerning the ministry

1. In the first part of the Lima statement concerning the ministry, "The Calling of the Whole People of God", the church is spoken of in the widest sense. The following tendencies in the understanding of the church may be clearly discerned:
1) it is open for a universalistic interpretation, which in the final analysis regards the whole of humanity as the people of God;
2) in brotherly love, solidarity is expressed with the oppressed, a solidarity which in the mind of a theology of revolution calls for active struggle against unjust social structures;
3) faith retreats behind the gifts of the Spirit that are enumerated.

2. The second part, "The Church and the Ordained Ministry", continues the charismatic tendency to the extent that the rite of ordination practically means only the confirmation of the gifts of the Spirit already present. So, one must be careful not to applaud such a development merely because one is committed to a one-sided Protestant understanding of the ministry, and so has no other concern but that ordination does not take on the nature of a sacrament.

Behind it lies the fundamental separation of word and Spirit, which has been the mark of enthusiasts at all times in church history. However, the statements concerning "Ordained Ministry and Priesthood" can only be welcomed. The grounds for the service of women in the ministry are weak, which is not surprising in view of the fact that almost all Protestant member churches have opened the ministerial office to women and have to find a theological foundation for it subsequently. Who can really accept the argument by which the picture of a new humanity in Christ is used to legitimate theologically the ministry of women in the church (Gal. 3:28)?

3. In part three, "The Form of the Ordained Ministry", the thought begins with the triple office of bishop, presbyter, and deacon, which can

be demonstrated to have existed in the early church. But the differences which are mentioned are understood in a purely functional way, and are declared to stand in need of reform. It is really expected that in this way ancient structures of ministry will be broken up, structures which are undoubtedly part of the essence of the church for Orthodox churches.

4. In part IV, "Succession in the Apostolic Tradition", a distinction is made between "apostolic tradition in the church" and "succession of the apostolic ministry". This is done probably in order to demonstrate, as far as function goes, a succession in worship and in the apostolic faith also in those churches which do not possess the apostolic succession in the traditional understanding of that expression. But can such functional definitions conceal the fact that fundamental theologico-ecclesiastical differences between the member churches of the WCC at this point remain unresolved?

5. The fifth part, "Ordination", using the pastoral letters as a starting point, describes ordination into the ministry as an act to carry on the apostolic commission, and deals in a descriptive way with the various stages of the act of consecration by reference to various ordination liturgies.

But isn't it taking it too easy, to describe the various ordination practices of the churches but at the same time to be silent about the fact that these are based on fundamentally different theological positions, which have maintained a church-divisive character to the present day?

6. Part VI is headed "Towards the Mutual Recognition of the Ordained Ministries". Here the purpose of the various declarations of convergence of the Lima document comes up. Without recognition of the ministerial offices in the "Protestant" bloc of the WCC by the Orthodox episcopal churches, there will be no complete church fellowship, certainly no altar fellowship. In spite of the almost imploring sentence: "Openness to each other holds the possibility that the Spirit may well speak to one church through the insight of another", it remains questionable whether the way entered on by Lima's declarations of convergence will lead to the longed-for goal.

EVANGELICAL CHURCH IN BERLIN-BRANDENBURG (WEST BERLIN) (FRG)

May the Synod resolve:

1. The Synod endorses the response of the church authorities to the "Convergence Statements of the Commission on Faith and Order of the World Council of Churches on Baptism, Eucharist and Ministry". It approves publication of this response and requests the church authorities to take appropriate steps to that effect.

2. The Synod regards these ecumenical convergence statements as a significant event in the history of the church, and considers their reception with both supporting and critical comment to be of general value.

3. The Synod requests church districts and congregations to continue considering these statements, the Lima liturgy and the responses to both. It is suggested that these texts be also discussed in interconfessional groups.

4. The Synod requests the Consistory, the Board of Education of the Protestant churches and the Ecumenical Missionary Institute to provide advice for interested groups, when so requested, in regard to their reception of the texts, e.g. with suggestions for further reading.

Resolution: approved by the Synod
on 18 November 1984 with five abstentions

Response to BEM

The "Convergence Statements of the Commission on Faith and Order of the WCC" (hereinafter BEM) were sent to all congregations and other church institutions, with suggestions on how to deal with them and with the request that a response to the statements be submitted. At the same time the Ecumenical and the Theological Committees of our Synod were

---

• 1,132,000 members, 12 dioceses, 166 parishes, 460 pastors, 36 auxiliary pastors.

entrusted with the preparation of a draft for the final response of the Synod.

Reactions from the congregations varied. On the one hand there was clearly great interest in the texts. Study groups were formed and meetings were held regionally on the individual themes of the statements. On the other hand only very few written responses were submitted. In general there was clearly less interest in systematic and critical study of the subject matter of BEM than in deriving ideas and suggestions from this ecumenical reflection for their own congregational work, especially as regards baptism and the Lord's supper.

Our Synod's Ecumenical and Theological Committees then decided to pursue this interest and take it further. Accordingly, in the work of these committees, the prior question was not what might have to be said in criticism of these texts, but rather how to formulate the questions and ideas our church has to tackle in the light of BEM. The results are not exhaustive but are governed by the degree to which we felt concerned. Where we have not given a specific response, we have nothing to add to the "Criteria for Responses to the Convergence Statements..." already published by the Evangelical Church in Germany. Generally the aim of our work has been to take a step towards reception, not to carry out a critical review, although we do ask some questions, and seek clarifications — relating chiefly, of course, to the third question asked in the preface, though our treatment of it also contains elements of an answer to the other questions.

All in all what we have to record is an ongoing involvement with these texts, which are of fundamental importance for the life and work of the church. We are grateful for BEM and are well aware of its great ecumenical importance.

Baptism

At present in our church we are facing the task of renewing our awareness of the gift of baptism and giving it greater emphasis in the life of our congregations. In our work on this we shall be paying special heed to the following suggestions of BEM:

1. BEM lends support to our efforts to give better expression to the meaning of baptism as "incorporation into the body of Christ". The sentence: "Through baptism, Christians are brought into union with Christ, with each other and with the Church of every time and place" (6) does correspond to our tradition; we nevertheless have difficulty in giving full prominence to the aspect of union (German text of II.D has *Gemeinschaft*, i.e. community/communion/fellowship: translator's note) with

each other and with the church. The reason for this is that there are many members who still regard baptism pre-eminently as a family church ceremony. It does already happen in many congregations that baptism is "normally... administered during public worship" (22). And in many congregations there are also extra special baptismal services, e.g. on Easter Eve (cf. 23). Generally, however, there will still be a need for deep reflection on the meaning of baptism, if it is to be firmly fixed in the minds of members of a congregation as incorporation in a specific community.

2. In our church too there have been years of discussion on the problems of infant and adult baptism. Although the terms "infant baptism" and "believers' baptism" are not appropriate to our discussion without qualification, the statements in points 8 and 12 do represent an enrichment of it. Currently we are working on a new baptismal order in which it will be stated that the church invites people of any age to be baptized. Our aim in this is that congregations should come to accept the baptism of catechumens — which is practised with increasing frequency — in the same way as the baptism of infants. Thus we endorse the sentence in commentary 12 that "the differences between infant and believers' baptism become less sharp when it is recognized that both forms of baptism embody God's own initiative in Christ and express a response of faith made within the believing community".

3. As to infant baptism, we accept that "Christian nurture" should be "directed to the eliciting of" a "confession" (12). In practice, of course, we shall repeatedly have to check whether the many kinds of effort we make towards a Christian upbringing in religious instruction and in confirmation classes, in day nurseries and play-groups, are linked in this way with baptism. We are also thinking about how we can arrange for the participation of baptized children in the Lord's supper. Up to the present we have encouraged the participation of baptized children of Christian parents in the Lord's supper only after previous instruction and when accompanied by their parents. BEM suggests going farther in this direction (comm. 14).

4. We too feel the need "to express more visibly the fact that children are placed under the protection of God's grace" (16), and some ministers and members are thinking about the presentation and blessing of infants or children in an act of worship (cf. 11) prior to the administration of baptism. The predominant opinion, however, is that to introduce a new act of worship as an alternative to the baptism of infants will not help towards an understanding of baptism and what it bestows.

5. On the "celebration of baptism", point 18 reminds us that "the symbolic dimension of water should be taken seriously and not minimalized". Here the reference to "vivid signs" that may enrich the liturgy may be of importance for us (19).

As regards the elements of the baptismal liturgy, the "renunciation of evil" prompts reflection (20). It is true that this liturgical element exists also in our tradition, but often it is no longer practised. We shall have to consider whether and how this renunciation can be both reappropriated and made explicit as to the "ethical implications" of baptism too (4,10).

6. In our endeavours to promote in our congregations an understanding of the gift of baptism, we are disconcerted by the remark in Commentary 21 that infant baptism is often "practised in an apparently[1] indiscriminate way". On another level, we feel that this mode of expression also lacks clarity and, if meant to be generally applied, is not very considerate. In the light of our Christian understanding we cannot encourage "believers" baptism, as BEM apparently urges. But its comment underlines our responsibility to give clear and salutary expression to salvation in Jesus Christ through the forms of baptism that are practised in our church.

Eucharist

The section on the eucharist brings home to us the fullness and variety of acts of worship. Our communion liturgy and preaching do bring out the aspects of the eucharist that are mentioned, though with varying emphases, but they are still far from having impressed themselves fully on the consciousness of members. Part of the reason for this is our church's tradition of participating only occasionally during the year in the celebration of the eucharist, because of the great respect in which the holy supper of our Lord has been held. For quite some time, however, we have noted another development in our congregations. At present communion is already being celebrated every Sunday in most congregations, even if often at the close of a service in which the sermon is the main element. We shall have to give special thought to the following BEM suggestions if the recovery of the eucharist as a central event in worship is thus to be achieved.

1. In our church too celebration of communion is connected with the "thanksgiving to the Father for everything accomplished in creation, redemption and sanctification" by him (3). Less explicit are the thanks for God's present activity "in the Church and in the world" and "for

---

[1] Apparently: German has *offensichtlich* = (1) manifestly, (2) to all appearances (translator's note).

everything that God will accomplish (in bringing the Kingdom to fulfil-ment)". Nor are we familiar to any extent with the aspect of the eucharist as "the great sacrifice of praise", though the collection made during the service is of course often spoken of as a "sacrifice" by which we respond gratefully to the proclamation of the word, and we are also familiar with the idea that the individuals taking part in communion surrender or give themselves wholly up to God and to that extent sacrifice themselves. But BEM speaks with much greater force about the world's being "presented" in the eucharist "to the Father in faith and thanksgiving" (4).

This notion linking a universal thanksgiving, and the promise for the world, with the celebration of the eucharist is important as a stimulus to us to grow in our understanding of communion.

2. *Anamnesis* is also a live element in our celebration of communion, though we are thinking primarily of the preached word in the reference to *anamnesis* as the "effective proclamation of God's mighty acts and promises" (7). It is, we think, an important point that the great acts and promises of God are not only expressed in the sermon and made available for our benefit in bread and wine, but that they also require to be celebrated in the liturgy. Seeing that there are signs of a certain weariness with the sermon among many ministers and members, we shall try to gain a better understanding of *anamnesis* as a celebration of proclamation. Here § 12 is important: "Since the *anamnesis* of Christ is the very content of the preached Word as it is of the eucharistic meal, each reinforces the other."

3. There is something of importance for us too in the overarching movement from the world's presence in the eucharist through the "communion of the faithful" to our responsibility for each other and for the world. We are more familiar with the idea that the individual's ethic and that of society are shaped by the preaching of God's word which comes to us in a special way through the gift of communion. As *communio*, however, the eucharist directs our view to the individual's participation in this fellowship as someone with a responsibility towards restoring the world. We shall be careful to encourage moves already on foot in our congregations towards emphasizing the character of the Lord's supper as *communio* and towards encouraging mission into the world.

4. We shall gladly pay heed to the variety of elements of the eucharist (27) when planning our services and celebrations of communion. A number of them could enrich our worship. We therefore welcome the opportunity to test our liturgy "in the light of the eucharistic agreement now in process of attainment" (28). We are certainly grateful for the

statement that "affirmation of a common eucharistic faith does not imply uniformity in either liturgy or practice" (28). That is also true within our own church. We are familiar with richly embellished communion services but also, for instance, with simple celebrations at a sickbed, where only a few of the elements listed for celebrating the eucharist can be discerned. But we believe that Christ is present in the one just as he is in the other.

5. Some of the BEM statements will cause us difficulty when it comes to ecumenical learning. Among these are the following:

a) "Its celebration continues as the central act of the Church's worship" (1). We cannot see how this statement squares with what is said in point 3, viz. that the eucharist "always includes both word and sacrament". We too could in one way describe the eucharist as the central act of worship, if we may take "eucharist" to mean our service of holy communion and compare it (say) with funeral and marriage services and various other occasions for worship including spiritual worship in our daily lives. Or is the description "the central act of the Church's worship" intended to suggest a higher value in this sacrament as against all the other elements in worship, so that one would for instance be obliged to attribute a lower spiritual quality to a service with no communion? As we see it, we are not free to make such stipulations about what is the central element in worship, given the New Testament witness regarding the power of the word of God that is proclaimed and heard.

b) There seems to be a discrepancy between the statement that "the eucharist is entirely the gift of God" (2,26) and the description of the eucharist as a liturgical celebration in which the congregation acts. Of course we too believe that Christ makes himself present in thanksgiving, memorial, invocation and communion, but it seems to us that the character of the gift — which is that we are first and foremost addressed and recipients — does not adequately come out.

c) What is said about the effect of the eucharist is not to our mind clear enough: "Through the eucharist the all-renewing grace of God penetrates and restores human personality and dignity" (20).

In our tradition it is stressed that in communion we receive "the assurance of the forgiveness of sins" (2); faith is deepened (cf. 30) and responsibility for service in the world is thus undergirded. In this way the Lord's supper also aims in our view at the renewal of persons — in their relationship to God and the world.

We are not quite clear whether in the text quoted it is intended to assert that the sacrament has the effect of restoring the human person and human dignity in yet another way.

Ministry

Since in our reflections on understanding the ministries and services in our church we too "work from the perspective of the calling of the whole people of God" (6), the approach here has our full agreement. We are also glad to note the content of what is said on the calling of the people of God. Here of course we are not wholly clear whether the same concept of calling can hold good for "the whole human race" (1) and whether in addition to proclaiming the kingdom of God the church is also called to "prefigure" it (4). For us however it is much more difficult to live in accordance with this calling, for as a church in a city where the process of secularization is making ever greater headway, we have to be constantly considering how our calling can be implemented "by announcing the Gospel to the world", and how members of the church can be enabled "to confess their faith and give account of their hope" (4). And there are also considerable uncertainties among us regarding the task of "(struggling) with the oppressed towards that freedom and dignity promised with the coming of the Kingdom" (4). In view of the numerous diaconal and state organizations for helping the weak, many members do not link this participation in social problems with the authentic mission of the church, even although they "seek to witness in caring love" (4). Nor is there sufficient awareness among us that the gifts (bestowed by the Holy Spirit) on the individual are given "for the common good of the whole people". Consequently many gifts that could be "manifested in acts of service within the community and to the world" (5) are insufficiently developed.

Turning to the question of the "place and forms of the ordained ministry", we have this "calling of the whole people of God" in mind, but also the as yet unsolved tasks connected with it. In this situation we take up the question "how, according to the will of God and under the guidance of the Holy Spirit, is the life of the Church to be understood and ordered, so that the Gospel may be spread and the community built up in love?" (6).

In relation to BEM we have to consider first and foremost the following points:

1. The basis for the ordained ministry and the description of that ministry call for specific reflections in regard to our office of the parish ministry. In §8 we read: "In order to fulfil its mission, the Church needs persons who are publicly and continually responsible for pointing to its fundamental dependence on Jesus Christ, and therefore provide, within a multiplicity of gifts, a focus of its unity". Given the burden falling on many ministers in the city because of the multiplicity of their tasks, such a description might indeed bring the subject into focus and to that extent

prove helpful. Since as we see it the task of pointing to the church's "fundamental dependence on Jesus Christ" can be implemented only by proclamation of the word of God and administration of the sacraments, the function attributed to the ordained ministry is clearly a limited one, though necessary for the fulfilment of the church's mission. We can regard the ministry of such persons as being also "constitutive" in this sense "for the life and witness of the Church", although the emphasis on the fundamental dependence of the church on Jesus Christ makes it plain that only he is constitutive for the church, while we merely have to draw attention to this fundamental dependence and bear witness to it.

2. Admittedly this helpful focus seems already to become blurred in §13 where "guiding the life of the community... in its mission and its caring ministry" is reckoned to be the "chief responsibility of the ordained ministry". From the programmatic statement in §8 one would expect that the ordained ministry would also, among such guiding functions, have the primary task of pointing to the fundamental dependence on Jesus Christ. In the commentary, to be sure, there is the remark that "all members participate in fulfilling these functions". But as regards the calling of the whole people of God and the challenge of our age we cannot see how far it is supposed to be helpful towards the fulfilment of this calling for the essential functions of leadership in the church to be reserved, to all appearances, for the ordained ministry. So far as we are concerned, of course, it goes without saying that for fulfilment of the calling we must recognize more clearly that "all members of the believing community, ordained and lay, are inter-related" (12), and that we should discover how they can help each other to deploy their gifts appropriately in their lives.

3. Mindful of our own tradition, we must respect the fact that many churches still do not admit women to the ordained ministry. But, according to the logic of BEM, the long-standing tradition of the church and "theological issues concerning the nature of humanity and concerning Christology" (comm. 18) must be measured against whether they do or do not serve the calling of the whole people of God in our day and in this or that particular social context. Accordingly, where it is recognized that men and women alike can discharge the responsibility of "pointing to" the church's "fundamental dependence on Jesus Christ" (8) women cannot in principle be excluded from the ordained ministry.

4. BEM recommends adoption of the threefold structure of the ordained ministry as an "expression of unity" (22,25). For us this recommendation raises the following considerations:

a) Since, to fulfill its calling, the church has to discharge diaconal, presbyteral and episcopal responsibilities (22), it is sensible that the ordained ministry should be a vehicle for these elements and functions. In our church this happens in so far as the bishop and the minister of the congregation discharge the functions mentioned in §§ 29 and 30. But in addition we have at a regional level ministers who are "struggling in Christ's name with the myriad needs of societies and persons" (31). They serve in a variety of diaconal establishments, hospitals and prisons and in the fields of education and nurture and therefore might well in the terminology of BEM be called "deacons". But as a rule they function outside the local congregations and their services of worship. For us, therefore, the suggestion that "the threefold pattern stands evidently in need of reform" (24) raises among other things the question how "the interdependence of worship and service in the Church's life" (31) can become clearer through the services performed by these ministers.

b) The same question arises in another connection. For alongside these ordained persons church workers provide services in a fully responsible way at every level of our church's life, especially in the fields of the diaconate, of teaching and of church music. While they are indeed inducted to their duties with prayers and a blessing at an act of worship, they are not ordained. In this connection we are engaged in a thorough discussion on the propriety of limiting ordination to a single ministry. On the other hand it is not the special purpose of these services to point out to the church publicly and continuously "its fundamental dependence on Jesus Christ" (8). But even if for this reason we do not ordain such workers, we understand BEM to be confirming our view that the quality of such services and ministries should be held in the same esteem as that of the ordained ministry. We should also have to look more fully into the way in which such workers ("deacons") can "exercise responsibility in the worship of the congregation", in order to make clear "the interdependence of worship and service in the Church's life" (31).

5. The description of the functions of episkope prompts the following reflections on our part:

Although in § 26 and in the commentary to § 13 it is emphasized that "the ordained ministry and the community are inextricably linked", it does look as if the function of episkope is in its full sense reserved for the ordained ministry. We cannot see how far this tie-up of episkope with the ordained ministry contributes more for the life and service of the called people of God than other forms of episcopal service. On the contrary, we think it appropriate from the standpoint of the calling of the whole people of God and its service in the world that those members of the Christian community who witness to the faith and practise love and service in the world in special ways — i.e. the laity — should have a fully responsible involvement in the function of episkope at every level of the church's life. With us this happens in the congregational council (presbyterium), in synods and among the church authorities. In all these bodies the ordained and the non-ordained working together have the same rights and so we can apply the term "collegial" more widely than just to ordained ministers (26). Notwithstanding this, of course, the bishop with us too has to "see that the Word of God is purely proclaimed and the sacraments rightly administered, and to be watchful that the Church is fulfilling its Lord's commission" (Standing Orders of our Church, art. 130). As the bishop also has to ensure "cooperation in unity and fellowship" within the church and has to represent the church in public, we too can say that he gives special expression to the function of episkope. But then again, the description of episkope as contributing to the unity of the church (cf. 20,23) reminds us of how it is frequently difficult for us "to express and safeguard the unity of the body" (23). As there is a good deal of diversity of opinion in our church, with far-reaching debates about how its mission is rightly to be carried out, it will be necessary for the sake of common witness to increase responsibility for the function of episkope at every level.

6. We agree with BEM in putting the greatest stress on the preservation and transmission of the apostolic tradition. For us, therefore, the witness of holy scripture is regarded as the source and criterion of the church's witness and service. In the apostolic tradition we can also discern the standard by which we have to test the establishment and structuring of specific ministries: they must be open to testing as to how far they serve the true apostolic tradition.

In our experience the due transmission of the ministry in the act of ordination does serve the interests of the apostolic tradition in that thereby a church member is expressly empowered to preach, to baptize and to dispense the Lord's supper. The person ordained can invoke this authorization even when challenged by doubts and disillusionment. As against this, we find that too little is said in BEM about the extent to which the episcopal succession is in the interests of the preservation of the apostolic tradition in the service and witness of the church today. Nevertheless we would be open to looking into the question of the use of this "sign" of the continuity of the apostolic tradition, if we can be clearly shown that it is of service to the fulfilment of the calling of the whole people of God, that it reinforces the apostolic witness and that it prepares the "way towards the mutual recognition of... ministries".

Theological Committee

CHURCH OF LIPPE
(FRG)

The 28th ordinary synod of the Church of Lippe (Lippische Landes-kirche) dedicated its meeting on 3 March 1985 at the village church of Heiden to deliberating the convergence document of the WCC Faith and Order Commission on "Baptism, Eucharist and Ministry" (Lima text 1982). They gratefully attended to the relevant paper presented by Dr Hans-Georg Link, executive secretary of the Faith and Order Commission, and with thanks they received their theological committee's vote on the Lima text. With few changes they transmit this vote as their *resolution* to the WCC Faith and Order Commission as well as to the congregations of their church. They see no final word in this statement but would rather like to encourage a further assignment — both on ecumenical levels as well as those of the regional church and of the local congregation. Specifying their answer the Church of Lippe synod declares:

It is with great respect for the fruit of a 50-year process of study that we received this document. We thankfully welcome the large measure of the achieved agreement and the promising convergence in which we see described a dynamics of moving towards one another. In view of the unity hoped for and to be coveted we confirm the statement of the 27th ordinary synod on the Accra papers precursory to the Lima text: the unity is to "comprehend the multiplicity of traditions, doctrines and manifestations of life of the various churches. Ultimately this unity is not feasible but is the work of God's Holy Spirit that has to be prayed for again and again. On the other hand each church is obliged to fix its own position in this process and to do all to remove the theological resistances and to dispel practical objections."

● 280,000 members, 66 parishes, 130 pastors.

We consider the Lima text a vigorous impulse in this direction for our congregations. In our statement we follow the questions of the Faith and Order Commission. We are asked:

1. How far can our church recognize in this text the faith of the church through the ages?
2. Which consequences can our church draw from this text for its relations and dialogues with other churches?
3. Which guidance can our church take from this text for its worship, educational, ethical and spiritual life and witness?
4. Which suggestions can our church make for the ongoing work of Faith and Order in view of this text?

Of course, as a church determined by the Reformation we can understand the first question only in the sense that we are called continuously to ask about the foundation of the doctrines of the church in the scripture.

I. Baptism

Ad (1): We acknowledge the effort of the declaration to describe the meaning of baptism according to the manifold evidence of the New Testament and to awaken the understanding of the other believers' concern by continually referring also their position to the testimony of the New Testament. We, too, can conceive the doctrine concerning baptism unfolded in the Lima text as a manifestation of the statements in the scripture. We appreciate that in the declaration no attempt is made to cause the churches and confessions to approach each other to the detriment of veracity. Each one is asked to reconsider his position in light of the central biblical messages. Thus the various churches by way of a critical stocktaking of their own position may approach the truth and thereby also draw closer together.

In accord with the declaration understanding baptism as "both God's gift and our human response to that gift" (§ 8), we emphasize that human response cannot be a second step done on one's own initiative but is exclusively enacted by the Holy Spirit and a response made possible by its work. In accord with the declaration we emphasize that baptism is an "unrepeatable act" and that any "re-baptism" must be avoided (§ 13).

Ad (2): If baptism is understood as the Christians' "basic bond of unity", we ask ourselves why there are divisions. We see their cause in our lacking the consequence of living as men who were baptized into the unity in the body of Christ. Hence all pastoral care may only consist in the call back into the oneness preconceived in baptism.

Ad (3): In view of the conception of baptism in our congregations we shall have to reflect still more urgently than so far on:

— how, besides the consolation for the individual, the idea that by baptism Christians are "brought into union with Christ, with each other and with the Church of every time and place" (§ 6) may be emphasized more clearly;

— whether with infant baptism the implications of baptism for faith and life are sufficiently brought home and whether the ongoing dynamic is revealed ("Through the gifts of faith, hope and love, baptism has a dynamic which embraces the whole of life" (§ 7));

— how, wherever infant baptism is practised, the congregation may back this so that the confession of Jesus Christ as Lord in someone's later life "is affirmed... by personal faith and commitment" (§ 15);

— whether the baptized children ought not to be admitted to the holy communion even before the catechumenate;

— whether besides infant baptism the baptism of adult believers ought not to be valued more highly.

In view of their practising baptism our congregations will let themselves be prompted to keep to the rule that the appropriate occasion for baptism is the divine service of the assembled congregation and to ask themselves whether the great festival occasions of the church are not particularly appropriate appointments for baptism.

Ad (4): We ask the Commission to consider whether they should not state more clearly that in the sense of *gratia praeveniens* the Christian church can theologically answer for infant baptism, too, and acknowledge it as a well-founded baptizing habit. We beg them to consider and, if necessary, to concretize the statement that "in many large European and North American majority churches infant baptism is often practised in an apparently indiscriminate way" (Comm. § 21b, cf. also § 16). We should not like to submit the admission to baptism more than so far to certain determinable conditions in order to refuse it if necessary. We acknowledge that we have to endeavour more strongly to give help how to realize the responsibility for the nurture of baptized children assumed by the congregation, the parents and the godparents.

II. Eucharist

Ad (1): We are grateful for the wide scope of biblical reference in which the declaration unfolds its understanding of the Lord's supper. The reference to the Passover feast of Israel, to the meals of Jesus during his earthly life, to his last supper and to the eschatological marriage supper reveals the Lord's supper in its manifold interpretations. The uniqueness of the Lord's presence in the eucharistic meal (§ 13), the singular and unrepeatable character of Christ's sacrifice (§ 8) and the understanding of the Lord's supper unfolded in the Trinitarian events are worded in a convincing form. Again and again the declaration succeeds in integrating also historical divergences in such a way that in this issue divisions need no longer appear.

Ad (2): Since the Leuenberg Agreement there has been a full community between the Reformed and Lutheran congregations on preaching and eucharist, which was then stated officially, although widely practised even long before. It is affirmed in a renewed way by the Lima declaration. In our dialogue with the Roman Catholic Church we are, in view of the Lima text, painfully aware that the common celebration of the Lord's supper is not yet possible.

Ad (3): The Lima documents unfold aspects of the Lord's supper which are hardly effective or are missing in our proclamation and practice: the eucharist as invocation of the Spirit which "makes the crucified and risen Christ really present to us in the eucharistic meal, fulfilling the promise contained in the words of institution" (§ 14); the eucharist as the great glorification, an event which brings not only *anamnesis* — realization of Jesus' crucifixion — but also anticipates his future glory; the eucharist as communion of the faithful, as "a constant challenge in the search for appropriate relationships in social, economic and political life" (§ 20). We recognize that the ritual-books used by us come nowhere near the full-scale interpretation of the eucharist and need reviewing. We suggest looking for visible and tangible tokens by which the sharing of community is demonstrated also in a visible way. Certainly the Lima liturgy may be a help to enrich the celebration of the eucharist liturgically and to more clearly emphasize aspects of the Lord's supper hidden or neglected so far. We beg our congregations to try this liturgy out. We shall have to examine whether these liturgical outlines give an impulse to the manyfold celebrations of the Lord's supper and which basic elements it contains which are new to us, which should not be neglected and which are to be incorporated also into our eucharistic practice. At the same time we shall examine whether the term "eucharist" can be applied meaningfully in our congregations.

Ad (4): We request a deeper consideration of the correlation between the Lord's supper and the proclamation of the word in view of the biblical evidence. So e.g. we ask:
— Are not many things said about the eucharist in the Lima text statements about the proclamation of the word in the New Testament?
— Can there be given arguments from the Bible in support of the statement that the eucharist is the central act of the divine service?

— Is the relative importance of confession and remission of sins maintained clearly enough in the context of the Lord's supper? Do not both
require a theologically more basic, ongoing consideration?

III. Ministry

Ad (1): The governing of his community is the work of Christ himself;
it is the ministry of all Christians to communicate his gospel in word and
deed. This central biblical idea is expressly comprehended in the declaration under I, which gives a decisive hint to the methodology of the
ecumenical discussion of ministry when the starting point of all question-
ing is termed the "calling of the whole people of God" (§6). Thus
Christians in their service of the gospel depend on Christ and on each
other. We learn from Calvin: "... If everybody were left to his own
resources and nobody needed the service of someone else (how arrogant
is human nature) everybody would despise the others and be despised by
them himself" (*Institutio* IV, 3 I).

This is why it is consequent to go on asking: "How, according to the
will of God and under the guidance of the Holy Spirit, is the life of the
Church to be understood and ordered, so that the Gospel may be spread
and the community built up in love?" (§6). On the one hand the
commitment of all this ministry to the one commission and, on the other
hand, the liberty of how to organize the ministry in fulfilling this
commission in various changing historical situations and social conditions
are safeguarded in this statement in a relieving way. This is why the
Reformed tradition — more clearly than the Lutheran one — recognizing
in the scripture an obligatory order of the congregational structure, said
that the Lord "sometimes awakens" ministries "according to the necessity
of times" (Calvin, *Institutio* IV, 3 I,4).

Ad (2): On this principle the dialogue with other churches should be
held and productively intensified. We gratefully experience the full
mutual acknowledgment of ministries in the Reformed and Lutheran
congregations of our church, indeed, theologically and juridically their
nearly identical foundation and structure in the constitution of our church.
That principle seems to admit a greater openness in acknowledging these
ministries, also outside the Protestant church.

Ad (3): We deplore that our church itself did not follow this trace with
the necessary consequence. We recall the declaration of the Arnoldshain
Conference in February 1970: "It is unquestionable and tragic that
emphasizing the authority of the preaching ministry and focusing the
whole of church ministries on this one ministry, and surely, last but not
least, the mass of parishioners demanding a certain religious security,

more and more resulted in shaping the image of the minister facing the congregation and of his spiritual status, both of which were generally accepted. However imperatively this aspect must be changed, this does not at all require a weakening or abolition of the ordination but rather a systematic correction of the image of the parson's ministry. It is necessary to differentiate the ministries of the church and to include the parson's ministry in them as well as to take the responsibility of the congregation seriously."

Ad (4): Sticking to this line of thought we do ask, indeed, whether the Lima document could really keep it up. Among a greater number of concerns we mention some which to us are especially weighty:

a) Can a formulation be admitted which says that "certain ministries are constitutive for the life and witness of the Church" (§8) in view of the fact that Christians as ministers have to throw themselves on Christ?

b) Are hierarchical structures on behalf of different spiritual qualities, as they are at least suggested in the Lima document (cf. §§29ff.), admissible in view of the fact that the ministers are and remain dependent on each other and on the assembled congregation? Must the statement be maintained that the presidency over the eucharist should be *intimately* related to "the task of guiding the community" (comm. §14)?

c) Does not the aspect of the whole people of God being called demand valuing more clearly the ministry bestowed on *committees* of the congregation and of the church towards individual bearers of ministry (councils, synods, presbyteries)?

d) Again, in many domains our congregations live upon the ministry (7b) exercised by lay persons in the light of their commission. Can such services be almost neglected in a declaration about church ministry (in the sense of "ordained ministry", §7c)?

e) Ought not conditions excluding the ordination of persons on the ground of their belonging to particular races, sociological or ethnic groups (cf. §50) to be refused more expressly as biblically unfounded? As regards the fully valid cooperation of women in the ordained ministry, should not those churches which have not supported and practised it up till now re-evaluate it anew in the context of Bible and theology?

f) Could not the critical questions concerning the apostolic succession being transmitted through the laying on of hands be emphasized more clearly?

We are concerned also by the principal question whether the church of Jesus Christ for its unity, beyond the essential characteristics mentioned in article 7 of the Confessio Augustana, really needs an agreement in questions of ministry as represented by the pattern of ministries?

The synod of the Church of Lippe endorses the suggestion of Prof. Dr Jürgen Moltmann "that to the Lima texts at hand a further declaration of convergence entitled *De evangelio* be added or rather be placed in front of it. It should discuss gospel-scripture-Tradition, Spirit and word, mission and evangelization and *ministerium verbi divini*..." We ask the Faith and Order Commission to consider this suggestion when reviewing the Lima texts based on the responses of the churches.

We ardently wish that by way of this statement the congregations of our little church may become aware of the possibility and chance to better understand each other and to learn from each other in the ecumenical context. What matters is "to realize and if possible also to experience that the others' being different is not a menace to one's own confession but rather an enrichment of the common profession of Christianity" (Hans-Georg Link). With such endeavour the broader basis of the common witness will become more visible. For the sake of this experience we should like urgently to recommend to our congregations to start discussing the Lima texts.

28th Ordinary Synod
11 March 1985

SWISS PROTESTANT CHURCH FEDERATION (SPCF)

Introduction

In 1983 a text, entitled in German "Taufe, Eucharistie und Amt" and in English "Baptism, Eucharist and Ministry" (BEM),[1] and prepared by the WCC Commission on Faith and Order after several years' work and various consultations, was sent by the WCC to all its member churches and to the Roman Catholic Church. After the Commission had adopted the text at its Lima meeting, BEM also came to be called the Lima document. The continuing worldwide consultation set in motion then by this document is one of the most important ever launched by the WCC. The present report in a sense sets a term to that part of the consultation carried out within the Protestant churches in Switzerland and is submitted by the committee of the SPCF to its Assembly.

The Lima document does not represent the results of a consensus-forming process but is a *convergence* document. The member churches of the WCC are invited to test how far the perspectives from which they see their practice and doctrine relating to baptism, Lord's supper and ministries are in harmony with each other. Within the SPCF we have therefore asked ourselves how far BEM prompts us not only to rethink our ideas and how these are put into practice, but also to consider in what respects it seems to suggest an approach the Reformation churches could not adopt without betraying Protestant truth.

The WCC had asked the churches to offer a response to this text "at the highest appropriate level of authority". According to the constitution of

---

● 2,836,167 members, 1,500 parishes, 2,500 pastors. The official texts of the Swiss Protestant Church Federation response to BEM are those in French and German. This is an unofficial English translation from the German.

[1] Translator's note: The German uses *Diener/Dienerinnen* (lit. "servants", also "ministers"; the second term covers women) instead of *Amt*, which is in the official German title of BEM but stresses the *office* of the ministry.

the SPCF its board is authorized to represent its member churches in the WCC. But neither it nor the Assembly are doctrinal authorities in the proper sense of the term. Even the synods of the cantonal churches are this only to a very limited extent. In our churches the highest authority belongs to Christ as scripture bears witness to him. He is also the highest court in matters of doctrine. When our synods make pronouncements on such matters it can be assumed that their decisions have much more to do with church order than with actual opinions on doctrine. If the Lima text were a consensus document, the churches would have had to express their views on it, as happened with the 1973 agreement on mutual recognition of baptism between Roman Catholics, Old Catholics and Protestants in Switzerland, or with the 1974 Leuenberg Agreement. But since BEM is a convergence document sent for comment the board of the SPCF opted for a survey among its member churches which would be as far-reaching and detailed as possible.

Our response is the result of this survey, which was one of the most comprehensive ever to have taken place under the auspices of the SPCF. It was open to all who so desired to participate. The results suggest that it would be in the interest of the churches to create a body, or a post, entrusted with stimulating and coordinating theological reflection among the Protestant churches in Switzerland.

Two different preparatory papers — one on baptism and the Lord's supper, the other on "The Ministries in the Church" — guided those groups who so desired to undertake the work. The third part of BEM, ministry, was the source of special difficulties, and for that reason we decided to devote a special working session to it. This was held from 22 to 26 November 1985 in the Le Louverain Meetings Centre, with the assistance of the Neuchâtel (Neuenburg) church. A great deal of work went into summarizing the responses and this was done by those in charge of the Theological Committee. Lukas Vischer undertook to process the results of the survey on sections I and II (baptism and the Lord's supper) with the support of a task force. Pierre Vonaesch, the theological secretary of the SPCF, compiled the summary of replies to section III (ministry) with the assistance of Hermann Vienna, and also drafted the record of the results of each session. The whole constitutes a summary report which — because of its scope — simply could not be properly debated within the confines of the Assembly. The board is however making it available to the delegates so that they can be fully informed in their preparations for the debate which will be made possible by the very much shorter report already at their disposal.

After some general remarks the present report tackles each of the three sections of BEM in turn. On each there is a summary of the most important convergences to which we think we can or must adhere, together with a list of those points where we either see non-convergences or find it impossible to subscribe to the Lima document. There are also some questions which we think our churches should pick up from the text, and finally there are resolutions on which the Assembly will have to reach a decision. These resolutions are so to speak the synodal medium through which the Assembly is enabled to respond — perhaps only partially! — to BEM.

Basic considerations

With the Lima document we find ourselves up against a basic difficulty in the way scripture is used. The SPCF has already expressed its views on this point in its response to the Accra text, on pp.5 and 6, 1.2 and 1.3:[2]

"It is somewhat hard to follow the document in its use of biblical texts. The Bible appears as a collection of timeless pieces of information, whereas it would have been more desirable to meet the biblical authors as partners in ecumenical discussion.

"Why are we led to feel as if the New Testament spoke about baptism only in one specific way? Why is there no mention of the differences which would take us back to the various authors, problems and historical circumstances. As the document offers the texts in detachment from their historical context, its pronouncements come to lack clarity... indeed to be incorrect.

"We felt it was necessary to give a better description of the way the primitive Christian community was able to live out the one baptism in the dialectic of unity and diversity, of unison and pluralism. The document leaves out of consideration the 'locus' where the practice of baptism and the problems associated with it arose and developed. It exhibits a tendency to generalizing theological formulations in which the specific historical contexts can no longer be discerned, either in the New Testament authors or in the individual confessional traditions of the partners in ecumenical discussion. It consequently is exposed to the danger of stopping short at a merely verbal consensus."

We can but regret that our reflections on the Accra document were not taken into account. With some small changes we could apply them also to the Lima document. We realize that we must apply the same hermeneuti-

---

[2] Report of the Theological Committee on the document from the Faith and Order Commission entitled "One Baptism — One Echarist — One Ministry".

cal yardstick as for the Accra text to the responses to BEM which have been received by the SPCF. Frequently things are not much better as regards the use of scripture in our churches. We are likewise prepared to ask ourselves whether we in turn ought not to have supported the present document with substantially more biblical references.

Our theological committee's study on the Accra text laid particular stress on the concluding paragraph's reference to the Commission on Faith and Order's desire to take the church's mission as it is currently to be understood completely seriously. One difficulty for us in BEM is that this very reference to the actual situation is largely missing. The accent is so much on unity that we are given too short measure on the theme "that the world may believe". We get the impression of a rather static and even slightly triumphalist picture of the church, portrayed in as complete detail as possible by incorporating different elements from the individual traditions. Admittedly no single tradition becomes the norm as a result of this procedure, but instead we find an ideal picture of the church, towards which everyone is supposed to be moving. This picture radiates a kind of timelessness as a reconstruction of the ideal church through the ages.

We note that in a country where most of the population has traditionally been Christian the question of baptism takes on a new significance in the context of increasingly recognizable secularization. It used to be taken for granted that every Swiss was a baptized Christian but this assumption is rapidly losing ground. Discussion about infant or adult baptism, on baptism as a conscious experience, on postponing baptism and presenting or blessing children is only in its early stages. So far there is no more than a rudimentary clarity about the significance that could and should attach to the binding nature of baptism in state churches into which people are born. It is therefore against this background that the proposals to our Assembly in section A are to be understood. If, as in the BEM outline, baptism can be seen as a process linked with a kind of renewed instruction on baptism (or catechumenate) on each separate occasion (§ 23), we think there could be some hope of increasing awareness about baptism in our churches.

The questions about the Lord's supper concern basic theological problems, but they certainly also have to do with the relation of our churches generally to liturgical questions. The churches in the west of Switzerland have been led to a complete rediscovery of liturgy as a result of a highly committed liturgical movement. There is absolutely no doubt that in the last thirty years a new sensitivity has arisen in them towards matters liturgical. In the churches of German-speaking Switzerland this development has not gone so far. On the contrary one may gain the impression that it would be necessary first of all to awaken an appreciation for meaningful liturgical forms which have developed throughout history. One seldom encounters the idea that the structuring of worship is not simply a matter of spontaneity and original ideas, or of affirming that the "letter kills", but could express the church's faith in stable but not rigid forms. The recommendations in section B cannot be candidly and critically taken up unless there is a positive acceptance of the church's need for forms of worship, and unless there is a realization that the church's faith is also transmitted in its liturgy, and in a particularly self-evident way.

In our changing situation we are having encouraging experiences with a diversity of church ministries, ordained and otherwise. We are convinced that the situation and mission of the churches must bring them to the point of not having to work with one structure of ministries recognized once for all as valid, whether threefold — bishops, priests and deacons — or of another type, e.g. the Reformed (Calvin) — pastors, doctors (teachers), elders, deacons. We acknowledge that the threefold office of the ministry does draw our attention to indispensable functions in the church; BEM has again let us see this afresh. We should however like to remain free to redesignate these *functions* responsibly as ministries[3] of the church in the service of the gospel and the community. The historical dignity of an office does not in our view lie simply in uninterrupted historical continuity, but also in taking seriously and positively the discontinuities in the history of God's relationship with his people. What for us is essential to the church, and so doubtless to the unity of the church, is not some ideal structure of ministries vested with historical dignity but rather the emphatic affirmation both of the uniqueness of Christ as the head of the church, and of the mission of the whole people of God understood as the "priesthood of all believers"; and therefore also of a number of people called by God to serve that same people of God.

Resolution

The statements from the Commission on Faith and Order hardly mention God's word and the proclamation of the gospel. This is where their crucial weakness lies. The responses of the various churches in Switzerland leave no doubt that this defect must be eliminated in any future version of these statements.

---

[3] Translator's note: German *Dienst* = *service* or *ministry* (likewise Diener/Dienerinnen= servants/ministers). The point of the suggested change is that the German text of BEM, e.g. §7, uses *Amt*, which is literally *office* ("of the ministry"). This it seems is too functional in the SPCF view.

The Assembly of the SPCF therefore in particular draws the attention of the WCC and the churches in Switzerland to the view of the Bible stated in the "Basic considerations" above and asks them to continue their reflection with these in mind.

A. Baptism

I. Convergences

a) BEM sees baptism as "incorporation into Christ". This view seems to us an important prerequisite for convergence. Many responses have welcomed the way BEM tries to express all the richness of the various understandings of baptism: through baptism Christians in their life obtain participation in the life, death and resurrection of Christ; this life is received on the basis of God's forgiveness, in it the Spirit is at work, and it is focused on the hope of the kingdom of God.

b) We find the conclusion drawn by BEM particularly happy: "Baptism is related not only to momentary experience but to life-long growth into Christ." Baptism really does initiate the dynamic of the Christian life and constantly reminds us of it.

c) In agreement with its view of baptism as "incorporation into the body of Christ" BEM says: "Therefore our one baptism into Christ constitutes a call to the churches to overcome their divisions and visibly manifest their fellowship"; it encourages the thought that "mutual recognition should be expressed explicitly by the churches". Serious doubts about this recognition emerge where some churches feel entitled to re-baptize. But where such recognition does not include mutual eucharistic hospitality is it not equally questionable?

II. Non-convergences and queries

a) In various places BEM seems even to attribute to baptism a force and effect which belong purely and simply to Christ. Baptism frequently appears as the subject of a sentence, as if the effectiveness to which it bears witness were contained in itself, e.g. in §7: "Baptism initiates the reality of the new life given in the midst of the present world. It gives participation in the community of the Holy Spirit..." We could not go along with such statements if they imply what in our view is an unbiblical and sacramentalist understanding of baptism. We suspect that baptism appears as subject because there is no section *de evangelio* in BEM and the presence of Christ in the word hardly comes into view, nor is use made of it.

III. Questions for our churches

Baptism and baptismal instruction are inseparable. Baptism itself, to be sure, cannot be renewed, but our recollection of it can. Baptism must be made part of our present experience. It would be good if congregations were more effectively involved in celebrations of baptism and if each individual could reaffirm his/her faithfulness to his/her baptismal commitments whenever baptisms are celebrated and on other occasions. Confirmation is one such occasion; it should not be the only one.

IV. Resolutions

1. The Assembly affirms the connection between *baptism* and growth in Christian living as set forth by BEM. It invites the churches to consider whether their baptismal practice gives clear enough expression to this dynamic and evangelizing aspect.

2. The Assembly agrees with BEM that "baptism needs to be constantly reaffirmed". It asks its churches to look together for means of bringing to mind the renewing power of baptism and revitalizing the related commitment to serve Christ.

B. The Lord's Supper

I. Convergences

a) In the chapter on the Lord's supper we can recognize significant elements of our own tradition. The Lord's supper is understood first and foremost as a gift. There is an emphasis on its character as proclamation, promise and the assurance of forgiveness of sins; also as the pledge of eternal life and as something received in faith.

b) We welcome what other churches have to tell us from their tradition and practice in celebrating the Lord's supper as this emerges from BEM. It can correct bias and faulty elements in our historical development and can remind us of the meaning of the Lord's supper as that was rediscovered in the Reformation. Here we are thinking of themes such as the joyful celebration of Easter, *epiklesis* (the invocation of the Holy Spirit), fellowship, reconciliation, sharing, and ethical aspects and eschatological and cosmic dimensions in the celebration of the Lord's supper.

c) We see here the opportunity to escape from unfruitful alternatives and oppositions, such as the polarizing of word and sacrament in which the Lord's supper appears on the one hand as a rarely occurring climactic event and on the other as a mere appendage in spiritual and liturgical life.

The various elements and aspects of the celebration can be seen afresh as an unbroken path leading us ever more deeply into the grateful reception of the gift of salvation and into fellowship with the giver himself.

d) In this context we feel it especially helpful that when the presence of Christ in the supper is referred to, the nature and mode of his presence in relation to the elements need not become a bone of contention leading to division in the churches.

II. Non-convergences and queries

a) We would not be able to go along with BEM if accumulated elements from the various traditions were to be reckoned essential for the celebration instead of recourse to orthodox church forms. Paragraph 27 and even to a greater degree the Lima liturgy give us the impression of being overloaded.[4]

b) Nor would we be able to agree if as Reformation churches we were not permitted to regard a service focusing on the preaching of the word as a full act of worship. In BEM as a whole, word and

---

[4] The eucharistic liturgy is essentially a single whole, consisting historically of the following elements in varying sequence and of diverse importance:
— hymns of praise;
— act of repentance;
— declaration of pardon;
— proclamation of the Word of God, in various forms;
— confession of faith (creed);
— intercession for the whole Church and for the world;
— preparation of the bread and wine;
— thanksgiving to the Father for the marvels of creation, redemption and sanctification (deriving from the Jewish tradition of the *berakah*);
— the words of Christ's institution of the sacrament according to the New Testament tradition;
— the *anamnesis* or memorial of the great acts of redemption, passion, death, resurrection, ascension and Pentecost, which brought the Church into being;
— the invocation of the Holy Spirit (*epiklesis*) on the community, and the elements of bread and wine (either before the words of institution or after the memorial, or both; or some other reference to the Holy Spirit which adequately expresses the "epikletic" character of the eucharist);
— consecration of the faithful to God;
— reference to the communion of saints;
— prayer for the return of the Lord and the definitive manifestation of his Kingdom;
— the Amen of the whole community;
— the Lord's prayer;
— sign of reconciliation and peace;
— the breaking of the bread;
— eating and drinking in communion with Christ and with each member of the Church;
— final act of praise;
— blessing and sending.

proclamation do not, as we see it, have a sufficiently high rating. In this connection the last sentence in §1 seems open to misunderstanding.[5]

c) Against this background we attach great importance to the following queries:

— Is it not a fact that in what is said about the Lord's supper word and proclamation are understood simply as preliminaries to the actual celebration?

— Could it not be that the "office" of the ministry acquires such a decisive role in relation to recognition of a celebration of the Lord's supper and to the unity of the church generally, because in the chapters on baptism and comments on the Lord's supper insufficient account has been taken of what the Holy Spirit does by word and proclamation to gather the people of God?

III. Questions for our churches

a) As to the individual elements that constitute the celebration, the *epiklesis* as a petition for the coming of the Holy Spirit on the assembled congregation should have an established place in the liturgy of the Reformed churches. On the other hand, original constituents of the Reformed tradition such as confession of sins and the promise of forgiveness should continue to be constituent elements of the celebration. The very rediscovery of the joyful character of the celebration can reveal a new means of access to them.

b) As a rule a person commissioned by the church should conduct the celebration, to make the unity of the church clearer both within it and outside it. This implies that other ministries in the church should also be actively involved in the celebration.

c) Because of their dual aim of faithfulness to the Bible and ecumenical openness, the Assembly wishes the expression "the Lord's Supper" to be used instead of "Eucharist".

IV. Resolutions

1. Celebration every Sunday is in line with the biblical tradition. As a provisional objective there should be an effort to achieve celebration of *the Lord's supper* at least once a month in each congregation.

---

[5] It has acquired many names: for example, the Lord's supper, the breaking of bread, the holy communion, the divine liturgy, the mass. Its celebration continues as the central act of the church's worship.

2. The Assembly calls to mind that according to the Reformed tradition the celebration of the Lord's supper follows the order appointed by the church for the purpose and is under the leadership of persons so appointed; but that does not imply that this celebration depends on an ordination.

3. The Assembly calls to mind the declaration made by the WARC at one of its General Councils (Princeton 1954): "The church has received the sacrament of the Lord's supper from Christ and it is Christ who gives himself to the believer. The table is the Lord's, not ours. We therefore believe that we do not have the right to refuse the sacrament to a baptized person who loves and confesses Jesus Christ as God and Saviour."

C. Ministries in the church

I. Convergences

a) BEM rightly emphasizes the calling of the whole people of God and their ministry, plus the fact that ordained ministers are supported by the whole congregation.

b) BEM does not make any qualitative difference between the ordained and unordained ministries and the ministry of the whole people of God, nor between men and women. We would not be able to agree to an interpretation which excluded women from service in one of the ordained ministries.

c) BEM reasonably points to the New Testament and its emphasis on collegiality in the exercise of the various ministries, with all the developments this diversity encourages.

d) We go along with BEM in recognizing that the people of God needs special ministers to cope properly with the demands of its general priesthood. With BEM we consider the calling of those exercising these ministries as God-given.

e) A ministry like that called episkope in the New Testament is necessary for the gathering together and the unity of God's people. Our Reformed churches seek to meet this need by their institution of presbyterial and synodal orders.

f) The threefold form of the ministry such as is known locally in Reformed tradition and practice is one of the possible ways of expressing the diversity that exists here. It leads to recognition of a diversity of ministries which is necessary for the life of the churches.

g) The way in which BEM speaks of the traditional ministries, and specifically of New Testament episkope, leads neither to an idea of unity nor to actual unity in the exercise of these ministries.

II. *Non-convergences and queries*

a) It is our conviction that the *representatio Christi* belongs to the ministry of the whole people of God and not just to the ordained ministers. We therefore regret the excessive value placed on the ordained ministers as opposed to the ministry of the community as a whole (the "general priesthood").

b) The way BEM appeals to history in order to present the traditional threefold ministry as normative seems to us to limit unduly the range of possibilities in this field.

c) Accordingly we regret the undervaluing of the non-ordained servants of the church in the overall picture of the ministers actually bestowed upon the church, as proposed in BEM.

   We regret that after mentioning the ministries of elders and deacon(esse)s BEM in the end absorbs them in the ministry of the priest alone. In its comments the text also neglects far too much the personal, collegial and community aspects which on its own showing are necessary for the exercise of this ministry.

d) The aspect of the ministry as vested in the individual is over-emphasized at the expense of the collegial and community side. One result of this is that a collegial form of episkope can hardly be positively accommodated.

e) BEM's presentation of the problem of the ministry hardly corresponds to the difficulties encountered by most of our ministers (pastors, deacons etc.) in the exercise of their service.

III. *Questions for our churches*

a) We cannot let the above convergence points (a) - (e) stand without challenging the Reformed churches of Switzerland on the overvaluation in practice of the parish ministry and the inadequate link of the ordained with the non-ordained ministries.

b) Our churches must grasp more adequately that the Reformed threefold form of the ministries implies an opportunity for their diversification and they must try to draw clearer practical conclusions.

c) Our churches must, especially in their legal documents, interpret the function of the episkope more clearly for their synods and synodal/church councils, and must give them the means of exercising these effectively at one and the same time in community, collegial and personal terms. The churches are invited to examine

the composition of the synods in regard to their spiritual and episcopal function.
d) Our churches should carry out theological reflection on the practical functioning of our church bodies, especially the role and significance of full-time chairpersons and secretaries.

IV. Resolutions

1. The Assembly supports the board's decision to change the title of the third part of BEM from "Amt" (the *office* of the "ministry") to "Diener/Dienerinnen" ("servants" and "ministers" — of both sexes). Jesus Christ in fact gives his church persons and not structures for its upbuilding.
2. The Assembly welcomes the definiteness with which BEM highlights the calling and ministry of the whole people of God. Its desire is that in the further editing of this convergence document those responsible in the Commission on Faith and Order will take more account of the unordained ministries.
3. The Assembly invites the churches to provide better guarantees for the diversity of their ministries both doctrinally and constitutionally and thus buttress the common responsibility of all members of congregations. It also invites them to strengthen the position of non-ordained as opposed to ordained ministers. In particular a higher value should be placed on the ministry of elders.
4. The Assembly invites those responsible in the Commission on Faith and Order to pay more attention, in re-editing BEM, to the circumstance that in many churches other forms — e.g. the synodal form in the Reformed churches — are a legitimate expression of episkope, especially in regard to their ministry in relation to unity. The Assembly further calls to mind that the church was born of the word of God. In the Reformed view the ministry of proclamation is constitutive of the church.
5. The Assembly invites the board of the SPCF to initiate reflections with the aim of arriving at a common view of ordination and induction in the churches of the SPCF.
6. For our Reformed churches there can be no grounds for excluding women from any ministry in the church. To this effect the Assembly invites those responsible in the Commission on Faith and Order to reconsider the statements in BEM.

Concluding resolution

The Assembly gratefully takes cognizance of the present report which was submitted to it after the conclusion of the questionnaire on BEM. It especially draws the attention of its member churches to the "Questions for our churches" and the "Resolutions" it contains.

It empowers the board to transmit this report to the WCC and the member churches of the SPCF.

Locarno, 16 June 1986   SPCF Assembly
Bern, 28 August 1986

EVANGELICAL PRESBYTERIAN CHURCH IN GHANA

I. BAPTISM

Lecture at the Pastor's retreat of the
Evangelical Presbyterian Church (June 1984)
S.K. Asamoah

A. Introduction

The Lima text tries to help all theologians of different standing to speak so harmoniously about baptism, eucharist and ministry for the first time in the modern ecumenical movement. The Commission having come to a common agreement on these three issues referred the agreed understanding to member churches to react to the following:

a) the central belief of the church or to what extent this belief has been maintained;

b) the faith of the church, that Jesus was born, died and rose to save man, as stated in the Creed;

c) how this text would improve upon our form of worship, ethical and spiritual life and witness of the churches.

These issues and others which will emerge during our discussion will help us to answer most of the questions especially on baptism, eucharist and ministry.

● 205,000 members, 710 congregations, 165 pastors. *Editor's note:* The Evangelical Presbyterian Church in Ghana submitted its official response to "Baptism, Eucharist and Ministry" in the form of several lectures by members of this Church. Because of limited space we have not included the lecture by J.Y. Ledo which is an excellent summary of the Lima text on the eucharist.

B. Institution of baptism

In the church of the New Testament times the ceremony of baptism was the only and indispensable means of becoming a member of the Christian church (Matt. 28:19; Acts 2:38, 10:48), the "ecclesia". It is one of the oldest ordinances that Christianity possesses. The baptismal practice was adopted by John and later by Jesus from the Jews because it was the most innocent, the most common and simple to understand by all. However, Jesus did not just adopt it but gave it a new meaning. It marks the end of the old life and the beginning of new life. The baptism of Jesus marked the end of his old life and the beginning of his new life.

It is therefore an enlightenment into the mysteries of God. Christian baptism is therefore rooted in the ministry, death and resurrection of Christ. It is a sign of making a new covenant with God through Christ and it is an assurance of faith in all that Jesus came to do among men, and would continue to do in the lives of all men who confess him as Lord and saviour.

Anyone who goes through this rite of baptism is committed to the Lord, physically, mentally and spiritually. He has become one with Christ. Jesus therefore is reflected in his thinking, behaviour and will.

C. Popular opinion

There are some popular opinions about what people think baptism is. In the opinion of some people baptism is a magical charm which acts on the baptized. Due to this magical notion people consider the officiating minister to be possessed by the Spirit before he administers the baptism, and the unbeliever has to go through some purification rite such as cleansing oneself from sex, a woman must not be in her menstrual period before baptism, and for some, especially for believers' baptism, fasting must immediately follow baptism. There is no magical secret in baptism. What is secret in it is the change from the good life to a better life which gradually evolves from a person. It is what we call *agbeyeyenono*, a new way of living, that is essential.

It is also believed that baptism wipes away all sins however long they had accumulated. People defer their baptism until their last days because of this, and sometimes families request baptism for their relatives at the death bed. In reality it is not the ritual which washes away the sin, but the gradual operation of the Holy Spirit within a person that can bring about change.

Some think that a person is saved if he or she goes through a particular form of baptism — either immersion or sprinkling. They claim that if a person is neither immersed nor sprinkled (depending on the preference of the believer), the baptism is not complete and therefore cannot be accepted as baptism. The emphasis here is on the form which qualifies a person for salvation.

There are some who believe that the mere act of going through the same process as Jesus did already saves them. What happens after that does not matter. This idea is quite misleading, for baptism is not a momentary act but something that goes on throughout the life of the baptized. Use the example of the farmers working on the farm — sowing and removing the weeds, thus enabling the corn to flower.

D. Meaning of baptism

Baptism is derived from the very word "bapto" meaning to dip, to plunge under water, to cleanse from defilement.

1. Baptism is a sign of the washing away of a person's sins in the name of the Lord Jesus Christ.

2. It can also be defined as a union with Christ to allow him to take possession of us all and as a result to grant us the benefits which flow from being likened to him.

This union indicates a sharing in his ministry, death and resurrection. "For surely you know that when you were baptized into union with Christ Jesus you were baptized into union with his death" (Rom. 6:3; Col. 1:27; Gal. 2:20; John 14:20; 17:22).

Baptism marks an entry into the new creation and during baptism the baptized becomes part of this. As a result of this entry the baptized give up their will and allow the will of Christ to work in them and declare positively their acceptance of the gospel message (Acts 2:41; 8:12).

Baptism is not only an initiation into the church but also into the kingdom (John 3:5) of God. The believer begins to enjoy or have a foretaste of all that can be found in the kingdom.

Another meaning which we can give to baptism is that it is an incorporation into the person of Christ. Just as in the first person Adam, unredeemed humanity in its selfishness must die, in the incorporation into the redeemed humanity of Christ all are made alive (Rom. 5:12, 6:4). The believer appropriates to himself the salvation obtained by Christ through baptism.

Baptism is a gift of God. It is the Spirit which helps the believer to be made new, and anyone who goes through this rite must be renewed daily. The daily act of self-examination is in itself a baptism. For example:

a) If husband and wife after many years of separation have agreed sincerely to come together they have been baptized in the Spirit.

b) A litigant who after discovering himself abstains from litigation, has been baptized for he gave up the old self.
c) The day those who sexually possess friends outside their marriage bond decide to abandon this unwholesome practice, they have been baptized.

Baptism therefore is a daily experience which runs through the whole life of the believer and the Spirit helping the baptized to grow (1 Cor. 12:3, Acts 2:38-39).

Baptism is participation in Christ's death and resurrection. At baptism Christians are immersed in the liberating death of Christ where their sins are buried. Paul compared this to the experience of salvation from the flood (i.e., Pet. 3:20-21). It is a liberation into a new humanity in which all barriers of division, whether sex or race, are transcended. The baptized is lifted above the limitations of profession, class and age that separate us from one another. It ends all segregation for in this both the poor and the rich have the same inheritance.

The following images can be used to illustrate baptism:
a) it is a new birth (John 3:5); the sowing and germination of seed;
b) it is putting away the old filthy clothes and wearing new ones in Christ (Gal. 3:27).

In summary, baptism is participation in Christ's death and resurrection. It is a conversion, pardoning and cleansing rite, a gift of the Spirit and an incorporation into the body of Christ. Essential in baptism is the conversion of the heart.

E. Baptism and faith

Baptism is both God's gift and the human response to this gift. If God by his grace gives us a foretaste (an experience) of the kingdom, it is the duty of the believer to respond to this gift, as said earlier. In order to make baptism more meaningful it is the duty of the baptized to continue to proclaim this gift through good works and firm belief in God. In baptism therefore personal commitment is necessary for responsible membership of Christ. As a result of this demand it must be renewed daily through self-examination, confession of guilt for past acts of sin and a struggle always to grow more closely to Christ (2 Cor. 12:2-8). The doctor and patient cooperation can be cited in this. A patient who refuses to take drugs prescribed by his doctor gets little or no improvement. This is what happens after baptism. Human response is necessary to growth in the Spirit. If the Christian grows he demonstrates to the world that humanity can be regenerated and freed from the bondage of sin.

This liberation and generation is operative in the church, the assembly of God's people, where there are opportunities to witness. During baptism in the church, it is not only the baptized who benefit but the individual who has been baptized is reminded of the vow which was taken before baptism.

Baptism in the new community reawakens the faith of the believers present. The gains of baptism go not only to the baptized but to all whom the Spirit helps to grow in the new life.

F. The baptismal practice

Baptism upon personal profession of faith is the most clearly attested pattern in the New Testament. However there was a gradual change in some churches to infant baptism in which children are baptized upon the profession of faith by the parents and godparents respectively. Despite this change churches like the Mennonites, Baptists and the Independent Churches practise strictly believers' baptism in which the person is asked to make a personal confession of faith before the baptism.

Although there are differences in the mode of baptism both have similarities. Both believers' baptism and infant baptism are mostly performed in the presence of their congregations and are administered to people from different religions. The difference between infant baptism and believers' baptism becomes less sharp when it is realized that both forms of baptism embody God's own initiative in Christ and express a response of faith made within the believing community.

In baptism therefore the congregation reaffirms its faith in the life and death of Christ and pledges to witness faithfully. It is therefore not theologically sound when during baptism the congregation sits unconcerned leaving only the minister and the participants to carry out this symbol of cleansing. Participation by all is essential at all times for it strengthens their own faith and the faith of the baptized.

If baptism in the church is accepted as valid, what then is the fate of those baptized in homes, hospitals and other places outside the church?

Another delicate point of discussion is about confirmation classes. If baptism as an incorporation into the body of Christ points by its very nature to the eucharist, do we therefore need another separate rite to interpose baptism and admission to the eucharist? If the answer is in the negative do we therefore have the right to debar baptized children from taking part in the eucharist which is supposed to strengthen the faith of the baptized?

Another burning question is when and where does the baptized receive the Holy Spirit. Some say that it is in the water. Others believe during confirmation or laying on of hands, while some think many days after baptism. Various answers to these questions cannot be disputed but what is real is that if the water is the symbol of cleansing, we cannot separate this symbol from the receiving of the Holy Spirit. Both work together to give the believer a change of mind to do good.

G. Mutual recognition of baptism

Baptism is an important sign and a means of expressing the baptismal unity given in Christ. Presently there are some churches which do not recognize the baptism of some churches as valid just because of either sprinkling or immersion. In order to settle these differences infant baptists must know that in the believers' baptism children are placed under the protection of God's grace through thanksgiving. And in the same way the adult baptists must also recognize the fact that after baptism of the infant the parents and the godfather take full responsibility of the child.

If this is understood baptism must never be repeated in any church. The first baptism is enough to strengthen the faith of the baptized through constant participation in the eucharist. In summary both those who practise infant baptism and believers' baptism must realize that both are valid in that children who are baptized are brought under the protection of God's grace just as the adult is prepared prior to baptism. What is necessary is the renewal of this sacred act in the lives of the baptized.

H. The celebration of baptism

Baptism is generally administered in the name of the Triune God. However it is doubtful if the early apostles were also baptized in this way (baptism was made in the name of John). The essential symbol of baptism is water. The use of water signifies continuity between the old and the new creation thus revealing the significance of baptism not only for individuals but also for the whole world. The celebration represents purification of creation. The baptized therefore have a renewed existence. Immersion, the first form of baptism, better illustrates baptism as participation in both the burial and the resurrection of Christ. And in baptism water must be sufficiently used.

However sprinkling emerges as a striking example of common sense and convenience over the bondage of form and custom. Sprinkling shows the wisdom of refraining from the enforcement of the customs of other regions and other climates on the unwilling recipients and shows also the over-riding authority of the Spirit over sacred institution. It must therefore be a clear warning to all societies, particularly sacred societies, not to lay too much emphasis on form or structure but on the kernel of the act which is the acceptance of the Spirit to dwell in the convert instead of stressing the mode which is secondary.

In the celebration of baptism the following are necessary: the proclamation of scriptures, the invocation of the Holy Spirit to be present during the celebration, and profession of faith in Christ and the Spirit. In baptism all that restructures the believer and renews him in God must be present and the believer made to understand that baptism is participation in Christ's death and resurrection.

The administration of baptism must be the duty of an ordained priest. However permission could be granted to certain people in times of serious illness to baptize. Baptism must be celebrated during public worship, for if it is publicly performed those present are reminded of their own baptism. Secondly, it gives the community the opportunity to welcome into their fellowship those who are baptized and to whom they are committed to nurture in the Christian faith.

Although baptism was administered in the early churches on special occasions such as Easter and Pentecost and is still practised these days in some churches, I believe the system must be reconsidered for all occasions of worship are of value to the Spirit, for Christ said: "Where two are gathered in my name I am with them." The Spirit therefore is present at every Christian gathering. Baptism can be administered at any place provided it fulfills the objective of converting the heart.

I. Baptism and new names

In making regulations governing baptism churches must emphasize the true Christian significance of baptism to avoid the unnecessary alienation of the baptized from his culture, through the imposition of foreign names. A name which is inherited from one's original culture roots the baptized into the culture and shows him the universal objective of the church. Names reflect the culture of many people. Names like Mawunyo, Sena, Elom, carry a better meaning to the believer than if he were restricted to foreign names which mean little and so make people believe that to be a Christian you must denounce the culture of your people and plant yourself in a foreign culture which is sometimes difficult to comprehend. It is not the name that changes a person but the Spirit of God which effects a change in the man.

J. Conclusion

In conclusion it is convincing to note that although water was used throughout the ages as the symbol of baptism, the emphasis was not on the water but the change in the new man. Stress must be laid on the creation of the new man and new society willing to be responsible for the caring for God's people.

This teaching offers us the opportunity to re-examine our confirmation classes. It seems to hold the growth of the believer, especially when he is denied the eucharist until confirmation. If the objective of this study is to create a new humanity and a new human society there is much for us to do, especially in bringing home to our people the meaning of Christian baptism, eucharist and ministry.

II. EUCHARIST

*Lecture at the 43rd Synod of the
Evangelical Presbyterian Church
Setry Nyomi*

The Christian family has a celebration that provides a focus of family togetherness. This celebration can be likened to the role an annual family meal plays in the lives of a close family. This celebration is called the eucharist, the holy communion or the Lord's supper.

It is clear that with families that celebrate periodic get-togethers such celebrations flow from their belonging to one family. For the Christian family, too, the eucharist flows from what ushers them into the Christian family — baptism. To refresh our memories, baptism is the symbol of a turn around — a turn around from the old life to the New Life. Baptism is the external act that shows that the internal change has taken place and a person has been admitted into the Christian family to begin a new life. This new life must be nourished and reinforced. This role is played mainly by the word and the eucharist. The eucharist is the ritual that our Lord Jesus Christ instituted to remind us of baptism and to nourish our new life. The eucharist could be described as a fellowship meal — a meal of all those who have entered into the new life. It symbolizes Jesus as the new paschal Lamb of the Jewish Passover. Since participation in the eucharist reinforces our new life, we can talk about it as the fertilizer of our Christian life just as the fertilizer aids the growth of the new tree.

The meaning of the eucharist

I. Before one can fully appreciate the meaning as clarified in the Lima text, one needs to outline a few common conceptions of what the eucharist means to a cross-section of Evangelical Presbyterian Church members:

1) a means of spiritual renewal;
2) a means by which the believer's faith is strengthened;
3) a factor by which we are united with God;
4) there is something magical about it; the elements possess supernatural therapeutic effects on physical ailments, etc.;
5) because in the Evangelical Presbyterian Church financial pledges are paid around the holy communion time, some people think of the eucharist as the time that the church gathers in money for its operations (a time that pastors collect their money);
6) a sign that you are a true member of the church.

Of course not all of these meanings are valid. Differences must be made between the valid conceptions and the misconceptions.

II. The "Baptism, Eucharist and Ministry" document agreed on in Lima outlines for us the meaning of the eucharist which is acceptable for all WCC member churches as follows:

It is the ritual through which baptized Christians strengthen the new life. Christians become more aware of the new life when we partake in it.

The eucharist is thanksgiving to God for all He has created and what He has accomplished for us, especially in reconciling the world to himself through Christ. One can liken it to the traditional festival "Dzawuwu".

The eucharist is also a remembrance (*anamnesis*) of Christ. In partaking in the eucharist, we remember effectively the sacrifice of Jesus Christ for the sins of all humankind. For Anlos, the image of Hogbetsotso brings this point home. As year by year people come home to celebrate Hogbetsotso, they do so in remembrance of how their ancestors escaped from Notsie. A move from slavery into freedom. The eucharist reminds us vividly of how we have been redeemed from slavery into freedom.

The eucharist is a means of asking God's Holy Spirit to be with us. The eucharist is communion of the faithful. Sharing at the table, even in ordinary life, is having communion (fellowship) with one another. Many traditional festivals are never deemed complete without communal meals. In the same way, in the eucharist, Christian participants also affirm that we are together a community of God. In traditional communal meal times, people whose activities destroy the community or family are either excluded or they themselves feel so uneasy that they do not partake in such meals. If this fact is grasped then Christians who participate in the eucharist would always do things taking care of the interests and concerns of one another. One church would also do things taking care of the interests and concerns of other churches. Since the eucharist builds the Christian fellowship and involves all aspects of life in the community, partaking in it has ethical claims on people. Whatever destroys community (injustice, racism, tribalism, destruction of other people's dignity, etc.) is challenged by participation in the eucharist. Participating in the eucharist calls Christians into a community that requires caring for others. Thus the community is also called upon to take proper care of the needy.

In the eucharist Christians experience an enactment of what it is like to be in the kingdom of God, and glimpses of what the final consummation of that kingdom would be like. Participants are strengthened to participate in God's mission in the world.

Inclusion vs exclusion

There are some ways in which in every church people have been excluded from the eucharist. The common traditional disqualifications in the Evangelical Presbyterian Church are as follows:
a) baptized church members who have not yet been confirmed;
b) baptized and confirmed church members who are polygamists.
These two are actually exclusions laid down in the "Hamedodowo". There are other exclusions which are mostly personal to people who, as it were, excluded themselves in order to take the eucharist "undefiled":
c) women in their menstrual period;
d) church members who have had sexual relations the night before.
These last two are not universal in the church.

The obvious question is: "Is there any justification for excluding church members on any of these grounds?" This question can be answered fully only in the light of the meaning of the eucharist.

In view of the meanings given to the eucharist above, what justification does a person have in excluding some baptized people? This is a very important question that the Evangelical Presbyterian Church should give careful thought to. One can argue that unconfirmed children and polygamous church members also need the nourishment for our faith so that they are not starved after their baptism. They have also been admitted into the Christian family through baptism and should not be treated as second rate church members or excluded from the common meal of the kingdom at which all Christians get strengthening. The issue of polygamy disqualifying people is a serious one when it comes to Christian churches in Africa. In Ghana, for example, there are several polygamous people who are serving the church in various ways and yet being denied the eucharist.

The biblical reference that establishes cases of exclusion is 1 Corinthians 11:27-32, where there is a caution against "qualified people" taking the eucharist in an unworthy manner (the BEM document also refers to this text). It could bring judgment rather than a blessing or strengthening. Again the BEM document establishes that participating in the eucharist has ethical implications. If these are ignored, the eucharist loses meaning and therefore can bring judgment rather than nourishment for one's faith. So, one could say that although baptism qualifies all for this sacrament, there is a caution for which some people cannot take it.

In the first category, given the meaning of baptism, one does not need to wait for confirmation before being allowed to participate in the eucharist. But one should definitely be able to tell the difference between taking it unworthily and taking it worthily. Thus a person should first be old enough to understand what the eucharist is and then how to prepare towards it. If a pastor can certify that a child has been taught what the eucharist is and could be helped to know the importance of taking preparation for it seriously, then he or she could be admitted. A practical question needs to be asked here: If children start partaking in the holy communion before they are confirmed, will there be any motivation for confirmation?

In the second category if the polygamous person was in that state before his admission into the Christian family through baptism, then he could be allowed to participate. On the other hand, if after being in the Christian family, a person consciously decides to be polygamous, then his/her admission will deny that the eucharist has any ethical dimensions. This is because that state is often one that destroys the basic units (the home) that form the Christian community and it thus challenges the notion of the eucharist as communion of the faithful. Admission of polygamous people in Ghana could also give a message to others that do whatever they like. This is not to say that polygamy is the biggest sin in the world. Based on the ethical dimensions of the communion, one needs to exclude known racists in the countries where this is common. One can also mention a few other such situations.

In view of this, therefore, it would be necessary to maintain this exclusion.

The other two could be valid only if attributing filth to things created by God and used the right way could be justified. So long as the situation does not arise from fornication or adultery, they cannot be accepted as valid exclusions.

Thus one can include all baptized Christians bearing in mind the caution in 1 Corinthians which disqualifies some of their own interests.

A look at our liturgy will reveal that almost all the elements listed in BEM E27 are included. We need to take a look at consciously including the following:
1) intercession for the whole church and for the world;
2) sign of reconciliation and peace.

For our liturgy to be in uniformity with the Lima text these two will need to be included.

The BEM document suggests that churches consider celebrating the eucharist more often than we do in our churches, since it deepens Christian faith.

In our tradition we do not emphasize consuming all the elements at the celebration. However, there is an encouragement to consider this, taking into consideration the ill and shut-ins of the congregation. The document also encourages us to consider taking it more frequently (once a week).

According to the New Testament tradition the church continues to attach greatest importance to the use of the elements of bread and wine which Jesus used at the last supper. But in certain parts of the world where bread and wine are not customarily obtainable it is now held that local food and drink serve better to support the eucharist in everyday life. Further study is required concerning the question of which features remain within the churches' competence to change before any decisions are taken.

It is hoped that with the acceptance of this document, Christian churches would gain victory over yet one more diverse tendency within its rank and move towards a unity of Christ's family on earth.

III. MINISTRY

*Lecture at the 43rd Synod of
the Evangelical Presbyterian Church
O.K. Klu*

I. The calling of the whole people of God

1. *The election of God*[1]

In a world of chaos God has called the whole human race to a life in which there is order. The call of the nation of Israel is for such a purpose as we are also called in a unique and a decisive way in his Son Jesus Christ.

By Jesus' life and service, death and resurrection, a new community has been founded which is nurtured by the gospel and the gifts of the sacraments. United by the power of the Holy Spirit in a single body all those who follow Jesus Christ are sent out as witnesses into the world.

---

[1] Arabic numbers refer to the paragraphs in BEM.

2. *The role of Christ in the election*

Christ's victory over the powers of evil and death, accomplished once and for all, gives the opportunity for forgiveness, repentance and deliverance from destruction. People are able to live a new life, forgive and love one another in Christ. Their minds are set on the day when everything will be made new with victory over disorder, and all will be in one fellowship with Jesus Christ.

3. *The work of the Spirit in the Church*

The new community or the church lives through liberation and renewal by the power of the Holy Spirit. Jesus received the Spirit at his baptism which empowered him to start his work as the preacher of the good news. This same Spirit was given to those who believe in the Risen Lord to carry on the work of bringing men to a life of order lived under the guidance and truth in Jesus Christ.

4. *The churches' task*

The church's life should speak about the type of orderly life we shall expect in the kingdom of God. By the coming of Jesus Christ the kingdom of God has come among men. Christ went about doing good and bringing relief to the underprivileged. Our life as a Christian community therefore is to bring to people freedom and dignity which is promised with the coming of the kingdom. In our socio-political and economic-cultural contexts the church's witness to Christ should bring relief to people. They would then have a foretaste of the joy and glory we expect in the kingdom of God.

5. *The use of individual gifts in the church*

Every individual in the church is given one or more gifts and abilities (1 Cor 12:6-7). All are called to discover their gifts and use them for the building up of the church and service of the world to which the church is sent.

6. *Divergent views on the call of the people of God*

All churches agree that their members are called as people of God but they disagree on how the life of the church should be ordered, especially concerning the place and forms of the ordained ministry.

In efforts to overcome their differences the churches have to work from the perspective of the calling of the whole people of God.

II. The church and the ordained ministry

7. Differences in terminology

Differences in terminology contribute to disagreements in the different denominations. To clarify your minds how the various terms are used in the following paragraphs they must be explained:

a) *Charism:* denotes the gift of the Holy Spirit to any individual member of the body of Christ for the building up of the community.

b) *Ministry:* denotes the service to which the whole people of God is called as an individual, a local community or as the church universal. Ministry or ministries can also denote the particular institutional forms which the service may take e.g. teaching ministry, healing ministry, etc.

c) *Ordained ministry:* this refers to persons who have received a charism and whom the church appoints for service by ordination through the invocation of the Spirit and the laying on of hands.

d) *Priest:* many churches uses the word to denote certain ordained ministers. The term is not universal. It will be discussed later in this paper.

A. The ordained ministry

8. In order to fulfill its mission, the church from earliest periods needed persons who serve as the focus around which the church revolves. They are responsible for pointing to the church's fundamental dependence on Jesus Christ. They help to direct the multiple gifts in the church to a united focus. Such people have been always ordained in the church.

9-14. *The role of the ordained ministry*: As people chosen and sent out by Jesus they are the pace and standard setters in the church leading the community in what they learnt from Jesus (Matt. 10:1-8; Luke 22:30, Acts 1:21-26, Acts 2:42-7). The apostles stand in a unique position and have passed on their experience in the tradition of the church. Christ continues to choose and call persons today by the power of the Holy Spirit into the ordained ministry. They serve as leaders, pastors and teachers, giving guidance and care to the new community under Jesus Christ the chief shepherd.

Since they serve to build up the community in Christ, the community needs them as people called by God himself and they remind the community of their dependence on Jesus Christ. However, the ordained ministry has no existence apart from the community. Their chief responsibility is to assemble and build up the body of Christ by proclaiming and teaching the word of God, by celebrating the sacraments, and by guiding the life of the community in its worship, its mission and its caring ministry. At the eucharist, Christ gathers, teaches and nourishes the church. In most churches the one who presides over the meal is the ordained minister.

B. *Ordained ministry and authority*

15-16. The authority of the ordained minister is derivative from Jesus who received it from the Father and confers it by the Holy Spirit through the act of ordination. To be set apart in ordination means to be consecrated for service. It becomes a gift to the church which edifies it. This authority is accountable to God and has to be exercised with the cooperation of the community. The ordained must, therefore, not be an autocrat.

C. *Ordained ministry and priesthood*

17. Jesus is the unique priest of the new covenant who has given his life as sacrifice for all. The church as a whole can be described as a priesthood. All members are called to offer themselves "as a living sacrifice" and to intercede for the church and the world.

By particular services the ordained minister is related to the priesthood of Christ and that of the church e.g. through the word, sacraments and intercession.

18. *The ministry of men and women in the church:* All human barriers are broken where there is Christ. Men and women can offer themselves for useful services in the church (Gal. 3:28). But many churches did not want to change the tradition of the early church so they continue to disallow women to be ordained.

III. The forms of the ordained ministry

19. *Bishops, presbyters and deacons*

Through the guidance of the Holy Spirit in the ministry of the church there emerged by gradual process three forms of bishops, presbyters and deacons, as the ordained ministry of the church. Although their roles have changed through the ages they remain distinct till today. The ordained ministry is exercised in personal and collegial manner.

At congregational, district and regional levels there is always the need for an ordained minister exercising a service of unity.

20. *Functions of bishops, presbyters and deacons*

a) *Bishops* preach the word, preside at the sacraments, and administer discipline in such a way as to be representative pastoral ministers of oversight, continuity and unity in the church.

   They have pastoral oversight of the area to which they are called. They serve the apostolicity and unity of the church's teaching, worship and sacramental life. They have responsibility for the leadership in the church's mission. They are the link between the Christian community in their area to the wider church and the universal church to the community. They, in communion with the presbyters and deacons and the whole community, are responsible for the orderly transfer of ministerial authority in the church.

b) *Presbyters* serve as pastoral ministers of word and sacraments in a local eucharistic community. They are preachers, teachers of the faith, exercise pastoral care, and bear responsibility for the discipline of the congregation so that the world may believe and that the entire membership of the church may be renewed, strengthened and equipped in ministry. They have particular responsibility for the preparation of members for the Christian life and ministry.

c) *Deacons* are referred to as catechists in some cases. They represent to the church its calling as servant in the world. By struggling in Christ's name they serve the myriad of needs of societies and persons. They exemplify the interdependence of worship and service in the church's life. They exercise responsibility in the worship of the congregation, e.g. by reading the scriptures, preaching and leading the people in prayer.

   They help in the teaching of the congregation. They exercise the ministry of love in the community and fulfill certain administrative tasks and may be elected to responsibilities for governance. By their leadership in cooperation with the variety of charisms in the church, the church has a link by faith with Christ and continues his ministry in the world.

Jesus is the ordainer and if we overcome the differences in understanding this, recognition can be given by all to all kinds of ordained people as participants in the ministry of Christ.

CHURCH OF THE BRETHREN
(USA)

I. The reception process and the Church of the Brethren

In January 1982, the Commission on Faith and Order of the World Council of Churches transmitted a text on "Baptism, Eucharist and Ministry" to member churches. Considered by the Commission "to have been brought to such a state of maturity that it is now ready for transmission", "Baptism, Eucharist and Ministry" was offered to aid the churches to grow together on these topics and so move towards the manifestation of visible unity.

The By-laws of the World Council of Churches state: "The Faith and Order Commission is to proclaim the oneness of the Church of Jesus Christ and to call the churches to a goal of visible unity in one faith and one eucharistic fellowship expressed in worship and common life in Christ in order that the world might believe." In 1978, at the plenary meeting of the Commission on Faith and Order, three elements needed for visible unity were identified: (1) a common understanding of the apostolic faith; (2) full mutual recognition of baptism, eucharist and ministry; (3) agreement on common ways of teaching and decision-making. Agreement on baptism, eucharist and ministry has been the focus of Faith and Order's attention since the First World Conference on Faith and Order at Lausanne, Switzerland, in 1927. These statements therefore are the fruit of more than fifty years of theological labour by Faith and Order.

The Church of the Brethren became a participant in these baptism, eucharist and ministry discussions at the point when the text was transmitted to member churches. The transmission of the text was also an invitation to churches "to prepare an official response... at the highest level of authority, whether it be a council, synod, conference, assembly or other body". The preparation of an official response was understood to

---

● 164,680 members, 1,044 parishes, 1,913 pastors.

be an initial step in a longer "process of reception". "Reception" refers to all phases of the process whereby a church appropriates the fruits of ecumenical conversation as integral to its own life and faith. It is a process that may take years, and only comes to fruition by the power of the Holy Spirit. The purpose of the "process of reception" is to renew all churches, and all Christians, in faith, prayer, and responsible witness in the world.

In Brethren polity, the "the highest level of authority" is the delegate body gathered as a congregation at annual conference to speak to matters brought before it. However, the members' voices are to be heard in conversation in response to the text before the annual conference delegate body in its representative role speaks. Accordingly, a draft of the Brethren response, received first by delegates to the 1986 annual conference, was commended to congregations and districts for study and response. In conversation with congregations and districts, the draft was reworked and brought before the delegate body for adoption at the 1987 annual conference. It thereby became the official response of the Church of the Brethren. And so the voice of the Church of the Brethren joins other ecclesial voices around the world in response to the BEM text.

A theological task force — Robert C. Bowman, Dale W. Brown, Dena Pence Frantz, Estella B. Horning, Melanie A. May, and Lauree Hersch Meyer — was appointed to articulate a response on behalf of the Church of the Brethren. In preparing the draft, the task force responded neither to the document as such nor out of Brethren life and thought as such. The focus of response is how "the faith of the Church through the centuries" is recognizable in the document to Brethren, who have received particular manifestations of that faith. We understand that all communions are called to be mutually accountable to our common faith and life in Jesus Christ rather than to assess the BEM text or one another by our particular heritage, faith and practice. By the same measure, we confess common membership in Jesus Christ's risen body, the church throughout all ages in every place. In our response, the Church of the Brethren seeks to confess the integrity of our faith and practice, to confess wherein we disagree, and to confess wherein we fear to lose ourselves.

The task force took guidance from the various responses Church of the Brethren members made to the text. A number of districts and congregations have made the text a focus for discussion. Insight sessions on the BEM document have been held at annual conference. Members of the Church of the Brethren have been asked to speak on BEM at a meeting of the religious news writers of North America and at various regional ecumenical gatherings. Articles on the document, authored by Brethren, have appeared in *Messenger, Brethren Life and Thought, Ecumenical Trends,* and *Mid-Stream.*

Brethren have also participated in the 1983 and 1986 baptism, eucharist and ministry conferences held in Chicago and jointly sponsored by the National Council of Churches of Christ Commission on Faith and Order and the Associated Chicago Theological Seminaries. Brethren were among the slated speakers and responders on each occasion.

The Church of the Brethren co-sponsored the Believers' Church conference on baptism in 1983. Papers delivered at this consultation are available in a book, *Baptism and Church: a Believers' Church Vision,* edited by Merle Strege.[1] The Eighth Believers' Church conference, held in September 1987, on ministry has been called by the Committee on Interchurch Relations and Bethany Theological Seminary.

II. The Church of the Brethren in Faith and Order conversations

The World Council of Church's call that communions receive the BEM document has occasioned reflection within the Church of the Brethren about the theological significance of these common ecclesial practices. The Church of the Brethren at once rejoices in and has deep concern regarding the BEM document. We rejoice that Christians confess with clarity and power that Jesus is Lord. Christians know ourselves bonded to Jesus Christ through particular forms of our denominational life and thought. Therefore, Brethren, as other Christians, enter ecumenical conversations knowing that we are called to be transformed, to be continuously converted. We find that painful. We seek to be faithful and open to transformation. Yet Christians know God's gifts, promises, and inheritance in the specific forms and realities of our histories, languages, cultures, hopes and memories. To be transformed means to be turned from what has been the bearer of God's life and fulfilment for us to what and how God is now giving, bringing, calling us to new life and service.

Our deep concern is anchored precisely in our joy. The call to speak with one voice as church challenges Christians to relinquish identifying our specific denominations with Christ's whole body as church. Our heads know that well. But we feel fearful. What if we should be called to relinquish that very inheritance which constitutes God's gift and promise to us? We know other communions also have such anxiety. That is why ecumenical conversations are so painful: Christians seek to speak as members both of our specific communions and of Jesus Christ.

---

[1] Grand Rapids: Sagamore Books, 1986.

The churches of the magisterial and Reformation traditions plumb matters of truth by looking to confessions, asking whether believers believe truly. Communions of the free church and contemporary traditions are more prone to look to actions, asking whether believers' confessions of faith are practised or not: believed enough to live or only enough to speak them. The Church of the Brethren, as other free churches, has historically validated faith by carefully examining its embodiment among believers.

III. Brethren responses to the text

A. Introduction

The Church of the Brethren shares with other Christians *that* baptism, eucharist, and ministry are central to Christian life and faith. From the perspective of our ecclesial experience, Brethren view baptism, eucharist and ministry as three expressions of one apostolic life. *How* we understand baptism, eucharist, and ministry reflects and nurtures our particular heritage and formation experience. Amid a hostile political and religious environment, Christian formation has characteristically occurred in the home. In such an environment, Brethren reserved baptism for that time when adults were prepared to live publicly as citizens of God's kingdom, even when that meant rejecting legally valid claims made upon them by political and religious authorities. Baptism was and is understood as ordination to the priesthood of all believers; all those baptized into Jesus Christ are ministers/servants (*diakonos*). All are knit together as a community constituted as Jesus' family, through Bible study, worship, prayer and mutual aid. All are reconciled to one another by the liturgy of reconciled service according to Matthew 18. All are renewed in life and ministry through Love Feast, which is preceded by feet-washing and the agape meal, and consummated with the bread and cup as solemn reunion together as Christ's risen body with Jesus' very self as the Life of our life.

Brethren believe others' Christian faith bears the image of *its* incarnate context as deeply as does ours. We have come to know God enters and is present to other communions and their traditions as powerfully as, but painfully different from God's presence in and claim on our tradition. One gift of ecumenical life has been the ability to see ourselves through the eyes of other communions. Now we can confess that our human need to define faith and practice normatively is just that: our *human* need. In scripture, as in the life of believing communities, God did and does not circumscribe to one expression what is the content of faithful belief and practice.

The Church of the Brethren brings our response to the BEM text believing we can recognize, receive, and be ministered to through the varied ecclesial expressions of baptism, eucharist and ministry. These ecclesial expressions manifest Christ's incarnate life, knitting together the many members of Jesus' living body, the church.

Church of the Brethren polity already allows for the reception of the BEM text. The Church of the Brethren allows for reception by (1) recognizing the validity of baptisms other than our own, upon a confession of faith, believing with the New Testament that there is but one baptism, a covenant with God to which God remains faithful; (2) opening communion to all committed Christians and encouraging members to participate in other celebrations of the eucharist; (3) recognizing the ordination of other church bodies and receiving ministers with the stipulation that the person understand and teach Brethren heritage and belief and be accountable to decisions and disciplines articulated by the corporate voice of annual conference while serving among the Brethren.

The Church of the Brethren has often been alienated by the language and life of the sacramental ontology that characterizes the BEM text. With other free churches, the Church of the Brethren has thought of itself as non-sacramental because our formation as church arose in embodying our affirmations of Jesus' living presence and lordship at the risk of death. But Brethren affirm the sacramentality of all of life. For precisely this reason, we find it inappropriate that Christians reduce to one understanding of sacrament statements intended to speak to our shared confessions regarding baptism, eucharist and ministry.

B. The Church of the Brethren, BEM and the faith of the church throughout the ages

In this section, we note wherein Brethren find convergence, have concern, and need further reflection with reference to the text. We find *convergence* with the document in the affirmation of:

1. Baptism as both God's gift and our human response to that gift. Brethren have understood that baptism is rooted in the life, death, and resurrection of Jesus and that as members are incorporated into Christ the reality of new life is initiated, indeed incarnate, in the midst of the present world.

2. Eucharist as the *anamnesis* of Jesus' death and resurrection in which Christ himself is present, granting us communion with himself and with one another as members of Christ's risen body, and as a representative act of thanksgiving and offering on behalf of all aspects of life, of the whole

world. The text's articulation of this rich understanding of eucharist as the sacrament of Christ's real presence has enhanced Brethren belief and practice, encouraging congregations to celebrate with bread and cup more often than at the semi-annual Love Feast.

3. Ministry as the representation of Christ in the way Christ himself revealed God, in and by commitment to the community of faith. Brethren have understood that ministry, especially ordained ministry, is not the possession of the one ordained but the gift of God's Holy Spirit for the upbuilding of Christ's body, the church, in the world. Ministers are therefore of Christ, though we expect Brethren ministers to believe, teach, and nurture our heritage. And when we worship with ministers of other communions, we expect to encounter their particular heritage, and through it, God's redemptive presence.

Brethren have *concern* about the document when it speaks of:

1. Baptism as "an unrepeatable act" and "re-baptism". As sacrament, baptism is both the sign and the reality signified. Concern for baptism's unrepeatability attends only to its sign (gift) aspect. Disallowing "re-baptism" protects the validity of God's gift and the validity of other communions' baptizing ministry. In this regard, we note the imperative, "must", in § 13. This is the only imperative and negative safeguard in the document. No similar imperative addresses the reality signified, the validity of baptized persons' committed discipleship as Christ's members. Making imperative the ontological while failing to address existential dimensions of baptismal sacrament constitutes a truncated Christology whose ecclesiology is able to clarify its concepts but is not equally compelled to indwell its confession.

Accordingly, we are concerned insofar as the text does not clarify and confirm the integral relationship between the confession of a believer and the validation of a community on behalf of that believer who comes for ("re")baptism. Put differently, the text is predisposed to speak of baptism in soteriological and/or sacramental language, without speaking to the Brethren understanding that baptism is a covenant with a community of faith and is, in this sense, ordination to the priesthood of all believers. One indication of this predisposition is the predominance of baptismal images of dying over images of rising into new life in Christ, as a member of Christ's body, the church.

2. Eucharist in a context that is quite different from the context Brethren find in New Testament writings and witnesses. For Brethren, that is, there is no *theological* difference between breaking bread with one another in the agape meal and receiving the bread broken and cup

offered from Jesus as eucharist. Brethren confess the real presence of
Christ, meaning the bodily presence of Christ as the congregation
rather than as the transubstantiated bread and cup. Baptized members
break bread to/with one another, enacting the priesthood of all believers. Although the language and images in this section are familiar and
indeed *could* be read as expressions of Brethren practice, the document
implies that eucharist occurs as individual believers come before a
priest. And although the text affirms that the celebration of the eucharist is "an instance of the Church's participation in God's mission to the
world, participation that takes everyday form in the proclamation of
the Gospel, service of the neighbour, and faithful presence in the
world", Brethren feel this section of the document nearly negates the
apostolic affirmation that the congregation, the eucharist community
itself, is Christ's risen and living body in and for the world of God's
creation.

Accordingly, Brethren are concerned insofar as this section emphasizes
eucharist as atonement without emphasizing eucharist as "a covenant of
good conscience" which rebinds the believing community to one another
in Jesus Christ. In this regard, Brethren miss reference to feet-washing
and the agape meal that are part of Jesus' legacy to us. Again we feel the
common quality of sacrament — namely, sharing a meal together and
directly serving one another — is de-emphasized while the proper
understanding and administration of eucharistic elements is carefully
addressed. What is spoken in this document carries the implicit weight of
being normative, and what remains unaddressed or unacknowledged
seems quaint, impractical, unimportant for the common heritage. Yet
feet-washing and the agape meal are part of the church's common
scriptural heritage. Our common scriptural heritage is richer than the
eucharistic discussion in the BEM text. Likewise, our Christian eucharistic life is richer than the concerns addressed in the document. Eucharist as
sacrament of incarnate life decidedly addresses concerns of hospitality,
table fellowship, and service.

3. Ministry so as to presuppose and perpetuate a sacramental and set-
apart understanding of the priesthood and ministry. Although this section
begins with an affirmation of the priesthood of all believers, most of the
section focuses on priesthood in the context of the apostolic succession
and sacramentality. Therefore, while Brethren could interpret the text
meaningfully, substantive consideration of the ministry of all God's *laos*
is almost entirely excluded.

Accordingly, Brethren are concerned insofar as the text intimates that
in the understandings and signs by which we recognize the formal

qualities of sacramental life, i.e., ordination, the unity of the church will be made manifest. Specifically, Brethren ask about acceptance of the episcopal succession as a sign of the continuity and unity of the church. Although the diverse patterns of ministry described in the New Testament relative to different times and places are acknowledged, this section of the text does not discuss patterns of ministry relative to changed and changing circumstances. In this regard, more attention must be given to the ministry of diakonia as well as to the ministry of episkope relative to the missionary call of the church in the world today.

Last, but not least, Brethren are concerned about the text's treatment of the ordination of women. Our concern is a testimony to the ways in which our life as a community of faith has been blessed by the ministry of women. Although we appreciate the reasons of caution regarding the ordination of women, especially with respect to our brothers and sisters in the Orthodox Church, we are disappointed insofar as the text did not treat this matter with as much seriousness as any other matter. Our deepest disappointment comes at the point where the text states with reference to disagreement on the ordination of women that "those obstacles must not be regarded as substantive hindrance for further efforts towards mutual recognition" (§54). It is our prayer that, just as churches refusing to consider candidates for ordination on the ground of handicap or race or class are called to re-evaluate their practices (§50), so all churches will be called into conversation around this critical matter.

Brethren need *further reflection* on:

1. The practice of believers' baptism relative to social shifts. In earlier eras, the common age for baptism, upon confession of faith, was the time when a young man or woman would assume adult responsibilities as a member of the community. We have not yet reflected on the practice of believers' baptism with regard to the fact that by the age of eighteen most youth no longer live in Church of the Brethren communities.

2. The baptism of the Holy Spirit. As an expression of solidarity with our Quaker sisters and brothers, we call for consideration of the baptism of the Holy Spirit and so for qualification of the text's rather exclusive emphasis on water baptism.

3. The reality that Christ's members may be stumbling blocks to us in matters of theology, polity, and practice. We confess our slowness to be self-critical and our predisposition to seek paradise lost rather than to open ourselves to one another and so to God's transformation wrought in ways we look not for.

C. The Church of the Brethren, BEM and relationships with other churches

Brethren have expressed our affirmation of faith by seeking ways to embody common faith. Our contribution to the church's incarnate presence in the world has been clearest in projects like Church World Service, CROP, Heifer Project, Volunteer Service programmes, international work camps, and student exchange programmes. Many of these were Brethren, and all were initially Believers' Church programmes, before they become common expressions of the church's witness to God's presently embodied compassion.

Deeply able to contribute to common enactments of faith, Brethren have been reluctant to engage in ecumenical reflection aimed at identifying *normative* understandings even of Christian baptism, eucharist and ministry. Perhaps the ghosts of our past have seemed too close. Believers' churches, in particular, came into being under threat of persecution. Both secular and religious authorities required conformity to their beliefs within their kingdoms. Too often Christians have created a trail of blood by conforming other believers to normative confessions. Christians of the radical Reformation refused to identify even the religious domain with God's kingdom as church. Subsequently, heirs to their radicality tend to mistrust normative definitions about faith far more than embodied expressions of faith. Brethren are more experienced at expressing our faith and practices embodied as action than we are in drawing believers into the gospel drama through liturgy or explicating the content of our faith.

The BEM text calls us to be accountable to our mutual membership in the body of Christ, thereby changing our perspective and posture in relation to one another. Although our faith is usually embodied as action, encounter with this text has clarified Brethren commitment in an articulation of our common faith. Encounter with this text has been an experience of renewal as Brethren have asked how diverse understandings and expressions of baptism, eucharist and ministry may be life-giving for all members of Christ's body.

D. The Church of the Brethren, BEM and worship, educational, ethical and spiritual life and witness

Three points in the text are of particular concern to Brethren: (1) the ministry of the laity, i.e., the priesthood of all believers; (2) the ordination of women, which is directly related to the first concern; (3) baptism as a pledge of allegiance to Christ, which is directly related to the role of the church in the world, especially in relation to the call to peace-making.

Basically, however, Brethren rejoice in the BEM text. We believe it fosters conversations among Christians. We pledge ourselves to join that conversation, knowing that in shared worship, prayer and study God will bring us closer to being the living church, the body of Jesus Christ.

Amid our deep joy and affirmation regarding this document, we do think it is but a beginning. Many Christian voices are heard and represented, yet many remain unvoiced. We miss for example the sacramental expression of Friends; we listen for voices of emerging churches with their concern for the incarnate, contextual, "human" side of sacrament and Christology. We hope to hear the voices of women and men from diverse racial, economic and social situations.

Brethren also hope for a more balanced sacramental and Christological expression in our continuing ecumenical conversations and statements. We believe greater attention to the Trinity will help us nurture the richness of our Christology. When we expect God's Spirit to call us to renewal and unity, we are more open to hear God's voice in unlikely (or even, to us, "heretical") places: as unlikely as the resurrection, as heretical as the confession in Acts 2 that God's Holy Spirit ministers through all who belong to Jesus Christ.

E. *The Church of the Brethren and the relationship of BEM to "Towards the Common Expression of the Apostolic Faith Today"*

Brethren question the normative role the Nicene Creed is given in the study of the apostolic faith. Formally the Nicene and other ancient creeds of the church have no place in the tradition and present life of the Church of the Brethren. The content of these creeds, however, is central to our understanding of the apostolic faith and our own self-understanding. These two affirmations may appear contradictory; they both belong to our formation as part of the radical Reformation, as we have both Anabaptist and Pietist roots.

The Church of the Brethren believes *any* statement on faith is a reduction of the apostolic faith, however significant those statements. We found and find in the New Testament a rule of faith and practice more adequate and reliable than any logically focused summaries of faith. We do believe statements of faith are important to Christians. We also observe that believers are prone to reduce the apostolic faith to treasured dimensions of their own heritage. Thus creeds as statements and confessions of faith are particularly prone to be interpreted in ways which defend a communion's investment, values and concerns. While the New Testament can also be used or abused in this way, scriptural texts which defy or challenge us remain part of our confessed inheritance and faith.

IV. Concluding remarks

Brethren are deeply moved and hopeful as Christians today proclaim that our trust in and loyalty to Jesus Christ calls us to conversion regarding how we express that trust and loyalty in relation to our specific communions. As noted above, Brethren have adopted documents in recent years which so amended our polity that we can already receive the BEM text. We are committed to unity in and as members of Christ's body.

Nonetheless, we remain concerned insofar as ecumenical conversation often seems to reflect a truncated ontology, emphasizing the eternal, the conceptual, and the homogeneous over the concrete, the experiential, and the heterogeneous aspect of our Christology. Ecumenical documents express great concern for achieving convergence regarding the content of faith. These documents seem less concerned with fostering attitudes and relationships which will enable Christians to engage in the reality to which theological convergence statements bear witness. The Brethren experience of ecumenical life, as of our own formation, is that convergence statements arise from experiencing together that we are made one in Jesus Christ by God's Holy Spirit. We therefore trust even the existential dissonance inherent to our particular historical realities, not only conceptual consensus regarding ontological signs, as we express our faith. Our cultural and ecclesial vision, therefore, is more heterogeneous than homogeneous; we receive the diversity that threatens to divide us as different gifts given by God for the upbringing of a common life.

We recognize that since we all know the fully divine only in the fully human contexts of our inheritance, our faith concepts are necessarily universalizations of our particular concrete confessions. But precisely that affirmation calls us to recognize that concepts and logic are primarily confessions to one another of the implications and limits of our incarnate heritages. Brethren confess that God's Spirit, not only our own committed faithful reflection, unites us in and as Christ's incarnate body, the church.

EUROPEAN CONTINENTAL PROVINCE OF THE MORAVIAN CHURCH

1.0. Foreword

The Moravian Church is grateful to the Commission on Faith and Order of the WCC for promoting discussion on such important, central questions of faith and doctrine by means of the convergence statements on "Baptism, Eucharist and Ministry" (hereinafter abbreviated to BEM). We consider this discussion, in our own church and with other churches and Christians, to be a necessity. We pray and hope that it will be the means of giving us new insights and a deeper faith in Jesus Christ, the Lord and Master of his church. Only as we turn to him can there be real unity in the church.

2.0. How we understand doctrine

It is distinctive of the Moravian Church (hereinafter MC) that they have not developed their own doctrinal system. Like the original Unitas Fratrum the renewed body has moreover deliberately avoided any rigid confessionalism. Nikolaus von Zinzendorf's *Tropenlehre* (doctrine of "ways") made it possible for members of the original Bohemian Brethren or Moravians (Unitas Fratrum) and Lutheran and Reformed Christians to have full ecclesiastical intercommunion without having to abandon their specific statements of faith. This doctrine of the ways in which God teaches us (*tropoi paideias theou* — God's ways of teaching), which places the confessions on an equal footing in relation to each other, has had a decisive influence on the theology of the Unitas Fratrum right up to the present time: clarity as to the basic truths of the Christian faith, openness and tolerance towards confessionally dictated differences.

In the "Basis of the Moravian Church" (*Grund der Unität*) of 1957 which is binding on all the provinces of the MC, we read:

- 18,235 members, 26 congregations, 53 pastors.

> The holy scriptures of the Old and New Testament are and remain the sole source and guide for the faith, teaching and life of the MC.... The MC recognizes the word of the cross as the central element of holy scripture and of all preaching of the gospel.... The MC hears the praise given by Christ's people in the confessions of the church...

These principles allow the MC an easy approach to BEM; on the other hand the MC does not find it easy to shape statements on baptism, the Lord's supper and the ministry that are typical of its own position: the attempt to produce a response to BEM can itself be an important and helpful exercise for the MC.

3.0. On BEM itself

3.1. BAPTISM

3.1.1. Baptismal practice in the MC

To the MC, baptism is one of the two sacraments; it is administered in the presence of the congregation in the name of the Father, the Son and the Holy Spirit. It is understood as visible incorporation into the body of Christ; the forgiving grace of God is promised to the person baptized. The water used in the act of baptism is a sign of the new life in Christ. For the MC infant baptism (the most usual practice), child baptism and adult baptism are possible.

The following characteristics of the baptismal liturgy are worth mentioning:

— the person to be baptized is baptized into the death of Jesus in the name of the Father, the Son and the Holy Spirit;
— catechetical instruction of children or congregation as the case may be is incorporated in the liturgy; this makes it clear among other things that the person to be baptized belongs to the congregation;
— a short address with scriptural exposition is an established part of the celebration of baptism;
— the passing on of grace received is signified by the laying on of hands by the officiant and the godparents and also, in infant baptism, by the mother (while the father holds the child).

After instruction the baptized child is later received in the fellowship of the Lord's supper.

3.1.2. Agreement with BEM

In the basic sections regarding the institution and significance of baptism (B1-7) the MC recognizes all the essential elements of its own understanding of baptism.

Specifically B3 and B6 correspond to special emphases traditionally found in doctrine and in baptismal preaching. Especially in the last two decades there has been greater awareness of the connection between baptism and faith (B8-10), not least because of the challenge of secularism on the one hand, and of a Baptist view of baptism on the other.

The MC further welcomes the references in BEM to baptism as something which establishes the Christian community.

On baptism BEM contains a series of comments and suggestions which call for reflection on the part of the MC. In B5 and B14 there is an emphasis on the action of the Holy Spirit in baptism, which hardly finds any expression in our liturgy. In B18 there is a call to take the symbolic dimension of water seriously. We should consider the question of the propriety of generally replacing aspersion, which is widely practised, by affusion. We should also consider which of B20's elements for a comprehensive baptismal liturgy are lacking with us, or are present only by implication and should be more explicitly identified.

3.1.3. Questions we would put to BEM

There is no point where we would wish to express direct opposition to the document on baptism. As mentioned above, there is a strong emphasis in the MC on baptism as rooted in the life, death and resurrection of Jesus Christ. This was important as against rationalistic and ethical humanist misinterpretations of baptism and can be of significance against new erroneous interpretations. We would go on from this to ask whether what is said in B3 might not be highlighted still more clearly with reference to the action of the Holy Spirit (B4,5 and 9) in the person baptized.

It is the spirit of the crucified and risen Christ that is at work before, during and after baptism.

3.2. EUCHARIST (LORD'S SUPPER)

3.2.1. The Lord's supper in the MC

Celebration of the Lord's supper represents the most important of all gatherings in the MC. In the signs of bread and wine Jesus gives himself to the congregation as he promised. The presence of the Lord in the Lord's supper is not to be understood with the mind but only with the "heart". How it happens remains a mystery. Members believe that Christ is present and experience his presence not just at the Lord's supper but also through "keeping company with the Saviour" even in the everyday world, as a reality that determines the quality of life.

The Lord's supper is:

a) a memorial of the last meal of Jesus with his disciples and of his suffering and dying for us — in the words of institution in the liturgy, and in certain lines from hymns;

b) a celebration which creates and bears witness to fellowship — this becomes clear, for instance, because the communicants eat the bread together (at the same time), and pass the chalice to each other, with hands thus extended to each other before and after the distribution of the gifts;

c) proclamation of the forgiveness of sins — the basic tone of the celebration of the Lord's supper is produced by the joy and thanksgiving for the renewed experience of forgiveness;

d) the link with the coming kingdom of God — especially, in the liturgy, through the reference to the "great supper" and so also to the connection of the earthly and the perfected community.

Celebrations of the Lord's supper in the MC are open to Christians from other churches. Among other things the church order says: "A particular ecclesiastical doctrine of the Lord's supper is not a prerequisite for participation. The participating congregation recognizes its unity in love with all those who come to the supper of the Lord as sinners believing in forgiveness."

3.2.2. Agreement with BEM

The MC is grateful that BEM on the eucharist has avoided detailed description of how the presence of Christ occurs. They are also grateful that the elements of joy and eschatological expectation have been expressly mentioned.

The comment that the eucharist embraces all aspects of life (E20) is of importance and we shall need to rethink it. This is brought out in particular by the statement that "all kinds of injustice, racism, separation and lack of freedom are radically challenged when we share in the body and blood of Christ". The MC should reflect more fully on the ethical consequences of celebrating the Lord's supper but without this leading to over-emphasis on the "law": in the Lord's supper it is the indicative of God's grace which is everywhere decisive and must forfeit nothing of its paramount role because of an imperative for action. But it remains important that BEM takes into account in the Lord's supper not just the Christian community but also the entire world with its needs and its guilt.

We should also be considering which of the elements in the eucharistic liturgy that are mentioned in E27 can be incorporated into our celebration of the Lord's supper, either as something new or in clearer form.

3.2.3. Questions we would put to BEM

The Lord's supper is a memorial and representation of the sacrifice of *Christ* for us. BEM says this too. But alongside this we find its reference to the sacrifice which the church should bring in the eucharist both strange and difficult to accept (E4). It is doubtless true that the New Testament speaks of surrendering one's life to God and in that connection of the sacrifice of praise and thanksgiving offered by the believer. But while the church's praise (E3) does of course also have its place in the Lord's supper we think it a deviation from the original meaning when this claims such prominence that it finally provides the name for the entire celebration (eucharist = thanksgiving). The Lord's supper is not our "offering and hymn of praise to the Creator". Praise, joy and thanksgiving are, rather, the sequel to Christ's gifts which we receive in the Lord's supper.

We also find it remarkable that, in the detailed description of the institution and meaning of the Lord's supper in El and E5-8, the forgiveness of sins, though indeed briefly mentioned in E2, is at most only implied. In consequence this vital point is certainly undervalued.

With the MC, the Lord's supper is regarded pre-eminently as a celebration in its own right and therefore not directly connected with other acts of worship even though frequently it may be only briefly separated from these in time. To us this seems wholly legitimate. When all is said, is there a full form of worship *as such*? Is it not rather true that Christ's people meet together in gatherings of the most varied kind, which only constitute worship *as such* in their totality and as part and parcel of everyday life. Now and then a service with a sermon and all the elements of the Lima liturgy (E27) may be appropriate, but if regarded as the norm for every Sunday it would lead to excessive strain on the congregation actually present (and not to thanksgiving!).

Finally, even in the age of ecumenism the MC would not wish to replace the term "Lord's supper" (*Abendmahl*) by eucharist. "Lord's supper" indicates that as invited guests we can participate in a "meal" (*Mahl*) offered to us as a gift — and the thanksgiving comes only after the gifts have been bestowed.

3.3. MINISTRY

3.3.1. The ordained ministry in the MC

The life of our congregations is marked by a multiplicity of services and ministries. In church leadership on every level — congregations, provinces and our church as a whole — the eldership, or the synodal constitution, is what counts. Alongside this there is the threefold structure of the ministry — deacon, presbyter and bishop — taken over from the Old Bohemian Brethren.

Doubts have never been raised about the importance of ordination as a sign of continuity and unity within the MC and of fellowship with other churches. The MC has nevertheless deliberately refrained from developing a detailed theory of the ordained ministry. Its church rules confine themselves to brief definitions about the origin and function of the threefold ministry.

The ordained ministry in the Protestant churches of the various regions was always recognized in practice. Many members of the MC belong at the same time to another Protestant church; that alone mostly ensures unquestioned recognition of the validity of ordination in the various churches where ministerial duties are being performed and at communion.

Along the lines of what is said in M29-31 the tasks of the ordained ministry in the MC can be summarized as follows:

A *deacon* of the Evangelical MC implements the calling of the church to service in the world as an authorized servant. By his involvement in Christ's name with the needs of society and of the individual, he illustrates how liturgy and diakonia belong together in the life of the church. He thus participates in the instruction of the congregation, in pastoral work and in long service. He has a share of responsibility for the gatherings of the congregation and is entitled to preach the gospel regularly and to administer the sacraments. A deacon of the MC is ordained in the fullest sense of the word.

A *presbyter* of the MC is an ordained servant of the word and sacraments, entrusted with a special responsibility for the spiritual state of the congregation. He is a preacher and teacher of the faith, does pastoral work and encourages members to live as Christians. Induction as a presbyter is renewed confirmation of ordination.

A *bishop* of the MC is a servant of the word and sacraments. Together with other ordained persons and the whole congregation he represents the continuity and unity of the church. It is his duty to carry out ordinations on behalf of the church authorities.

Since 1467 the ministry in the MC, transmitted in orderly fashion, has been understood as a connecting link with the ancient church. Its transmission, however, has not been regarded as an episcopal succession (by divine ordinance) in the Roman Catholic sense. In the MC it has never been taught that there is any essential differentiation within the ordained ministry. Consequently they can also recognize ministries and ordination in churches with no episcopal tradition.

In the eighteenth century there were many functions at a congregational level exercised in the MC by women. For a time this led to the *ordination of women* as "deaconesses" and "priests". Only in 1950 was the ordination of women reintroduced, after a lapse of two centuries. It is firmly established in the church order of the MC.

3.3.2. Agreement with BEM

For us it is important that BEM's starting point in M16 is the calling of the whole people of God. This is the basis from which the ministry as a special element can be derived.

In BEM there is a greater emphasis than in previous WCC documents on the threefold structure of the ordained ministry. The MC expressly welcomes this as it corresponds to its own history and also opens doors towards other churches. It would be grateful if the threefold ministry could operate "as an expression of the unity we seek and also as a means for achieving it" (M22). But it understands the reservations of other churches not living in that tradition. The essential unity of the church of Jesus Christ can find expression also with other forms of the ministry. The MC would highlight what is said in the commentary on M11.

3.3.3. Questions we would put to BEM

In BEM the sequence runs from bishop through presbyter to deacon. To be sure little depends on this sequence provided it is kept in mind that Christ is the bishop and elder of his church and also its servant, from whom every service and ministry is derived. We think it important to draw attention to the fact that even the ordained ministry participates in the general priesthood of the people of God, and this is more clearly expressed in the sequence we have chosen: deacon-presbyter-bishop.

4.0. The questions put by the Commission on Faith and Order

In the preface to BEM the Commission on Faith and Order asks four questions of the member churches of the WCC. The first three of them have already been answered in outline in our response.

The fourth question relates to suggestions for the ongoing work of Faith and Order as it relates to BEM. In the view of the MC, the Commission on Faith and Order should also continue to promote conversations between two or more churches, making use of partnerships that already exist for this theological discussion too. As a world church, the MC would urgently ask the Commission on Faith and Order to do all it can to ensure that the theological debate does not take place within Europe or North America or between them, but between North and South and East and West. The voices of the "young churches" (as they are called) must be heard.

The same holds good for the long term study project "Towards the Common Expression of the Apostolic Faith Today". We can make headway with the new expression of the apostolic faith only if the whole oikoumene, the whole of world Christianity, participates from the start. We ask the Commission on Faith and Order to ensure that African, Asian and Latin American churches likewise cooperate in these studies.

UNITED GERMAN MENNONITE CONGREGATIONS

Preliminary note

The Executive Board of the Vereinigung der Deutschen Mennonitengemeinden (United German Mennonite Congregations) has accepted the following statements concerning the Lima convergence statement as its preliminary response. The executive board explicitly refers to point I.2 of this response and does not regard this response as a final word nor as a church-official and binding declaration. The congregations will continue to deal with the Lima paper and this preliminary response.

I. Principle considerations

1. Differing conceptions of the Christian faith and life, as they appear in the different Christian denominations, lead in our understanding, as well, to the distressing question of the unity of the church of Jesus Christ. Therefore we appreciate and welcome the convergence statement of the Faith and Order Commission of the World Council of Churches. It broadens our horizon; we learn from the conceptions of other churches. We sense therein the serious and responsible endeavour to further the converging movement of the churches and to renew the vision of a visual unity of the worldwide church. At the same time we try to conceive of the difficulties the Commission must have had in working out the details. For there were representatives of various differing churches. When we now present a short statement on the Lima convergence statement, we ask the Commission to show understanding for our distinct critical position. We think that openness will advance the ecumenical dialogue and we hope that denominational traditions like ours will be stronger perceived in future publications of the Commission.

● 7,350 members, 40 parishes, 25 pastors.

2. Our difficulties with the Lima convergence statement begin with the request of the Commission to study and "to respond to the text at the highest appropriate level of authority". The idea of a highest authority is not known in our congregations. The thinking in categories of "above and beneath" is according to our understanding foreign to the nature of the Christian church. "You have one master and you are all siblings (brethren)," says Jesus (Matt. 23:8).

In our church each congregation is individually responsible and competent, even in spiritual matters. The insights of the theological layman contribute just as much to the process of opinion-leading, such as congregational meetings, as those of a theological specialist. Therefore it is our view that a discussion of the Lima texts is meaningful mainly on this level. But the texts presuppose the knowledge of a theological world of thought which is to a large extent foreign to the members of our congregations. The texts are written in a technical language of theology which stands in the way of being noticed, let alone of being received by the laity. Very seldom have we been successful in picking up the convergence statement on the level that in our view is desirable. But even if we would manage to translate it into a simpler language, we would need more time for our response. That is why this answer has been prepared only by theologians.

3. Another observation that may cohere with the one mentioned first leaves us with a feeling of uneasiness, as well. In the convergence statement there is so much stress on the traditions of the churches, more specifically those of some churches, that the relationship to the scriptures is suffering. We know that we agree with other churches of the Reformation tradition on the point that the scriptures must be the starting point for our faith and understanding, especially in their witness to Jesus Christ. For this reason we cannot attach as much dignity to the tradition of the church as other churches do. We believe to have understood that the church is again and again in danger of going wrong. Therefore only in returning to the gospel as it is attested in the scriptures lies the chance for a new beginning.

The church is according to our understanding always in motion, either towards Christ or away from him. The church attempts to be the church. In contrast, the Lima texts often show an understanding of the church that is hardly self-critical. In our own church and in the history of other churches there are unfortunately enough examples of the church missing her commission — and not only because of a different understanding of baptism, the Lord's supper and ministry, but also with respect to humaneness, solidarity with the poor, justice, and the relation to the powerful. There we believe that the traditions of the churches in regard to faith and forms of life must continuously be reconsidered on the basis of a new understanding of the gospel. To this end serves the Bible as it acquires new meaning and interpretation in and by the church.

4. The third point that we want to put forward in the first part of our response is related to the first two points. Our question is: At which unity is the Lima convergence statement aiming, when thinking in terms of authoritative-ecclesiastical structures is so important and when the traditions of some churches receive so much dignity? We ask that this question will not be taken as one thought out and formulated without love. With the stated question we want to express our concern that the unity aimed at by the convergence statement might become a unity of the big institutional churches (*Amtskirchen*), while the churches with congregational structures are not present in this "model of unity". But we want to emphasize that we are also interested in the unity of the church of Christ. However, we think that this unity must be described first of all as a unity given by Christ. We doubt that unity is "makeable" (*machbar*). It seems to us that it would be more appropriate to say that Christ is ahead of his church because in him God has reconciled all unto himself. The churches, however, interpret faith in Christ differently and come to forms of life that differ from each other. Out of these considerations we ask the Commission to reconsider the model of unity appearing in the Lima texts. Perhaps the model of the reconciling differences might serve better the common goal at this point in time. It does not exclude the efforts of reconciliation in doctrinal questions and in the practice of the churches with regard to baptism, the Lord's supper and ministry. Despite these stated concerns we would like to respond with the following remarks directly to the mentioned points.

II. Baptism

As a church that defends believers' baptism, we regard the Lima statement on baptism generally as helpful. Nevertheless, we have some questions and reservations.

1. Paragraphs 1-10, respectively 11, on the institution and meaning of baptism as well as on the relation of baptism to faith, we can by and large support. We especially welcome the explicit reference to the fact that baptism and faith are closely connected and that baptism is not only a gift of God but that it also carries the character of an answer to the call of God. We are thankful that discipleship of Christ as it follows from baptism is emphasized. We share the conviction that baptism must be

seen in close relation to both the local congregation and the worldwide church of Jesus Christ. Finally we support the repeated remarks that a life out of baptism always carries the character of growth (§ 9). A prerequisite for baptism is therefore, according to our understanding, not a reached and measureable "faith-achievement" (*Glaubensleistung*), but rather a willingness to follow God's call and "to grow in the understanding of faith" (§ 12).

2. Paragraph 7 of the Lima statement on baptism helps us to understand the doctrine of baptism of other churches better. We understand the appeal of the Lima statement to acknowledge baptism mutually, as a serious question put to our church. We know that our doctrine and practice of baptism have their problems, as well. For instance, the question of the appropriate age for baptism or the question of how the congregation can correctly judge the testimony of the candidates for baptism. When our congregations in case of a change of religion are faced with the question of whether to accept infant baptism in retrospect, we have no uniform practice. In such cases we are working towards accepting infant baptism, not only to avoid the offence to other churches, but also to counter the misunderstanding that baptism is only a human act.

3. Even if God's action always precedes the human act, the candidate for baptism's response in faith to the call of God shall not be absent. This individual response cannot be substituted by a "corporate faith" of the church. According to the statements on baptism in the first ten paragraphs of the Lima statement, we can only understand the baptism upon the personal confession of faith as the practice of baptism that is substantiated by the New Testament.

4. We share the opinion that children and minors are not excluded from God's salvation. In many of our congregations this is expressed through the blessing of children. Such a practice incorporates those elements which we accept as legitimate, but which do not substantiate infant baptism. These elements being thankfulness for the child, prayer for God's blessing, commitment of parents, family and church to be supportive.

5. Baptism is unrepeatable for us, as well. But the remark concerning the "sacramental integrity of other churches" cannot be the only measurement for the legitimacy of baptism. At this point we must reject a sacramental understanding of baptism, so as if it would work out of itself and would give it a quality that could not be lost, independent of human faith and trust. God's action in baptism has been invested in view of our response in faith and discipleship.

III. The Lord's supper

1. In §4 the Lord's supper has been given the character of a universal feast of joy and thanksgiving which is understood as "the continuation of Jesus' work, i.e. his sharing of the meal with tax collectors and sinners" (§24). We appreciate this view as enriching our own under- standing of the Lord's supper. In light of this view of the Lord's supper, we recognize a contracted view in many Mennonite congregations which we hope to overcome. In most congregations we celebrate too seldom. And when we celebrate the Lord's supper, we pose too often the limiting question as to whether the individual is worthy of it. But at the same time we are critical of the manner in which the Lima statement is expounding this aspect of joy. We see the danger of a triumphalistic over-emphasis on salvation and on the church which is mediating it. The cross has been levelled too much in the description of salvation history that begins with creation and continues in the church (§4). We appreciate that the Lima statement — though non-committal — points out the consequences of the celebration of the Lord's supper that ensue for the common life in discipleship of Christ crucified. The claim of the Lord's supper to be a feast of joy in the church can only be grounded in the willingness to live in discipleship, service and repentance. From our perspective, it is a reason for repentance, when many Christians have become martyrs as the result of the action of other Christians. In this connection we want to express that for us the term "eucharist" does not seem to be an appropriate generic term. It emphasizes unduly one, though important, aspect of the Lord's supper.

2. It has been enriching for us to see the Lord's supper as a "vision of the divine rule" (§22) and as a "foretaste" of the same. This eschatologi- cal view has as yet not been emphasized in our congregations. But the reality anticipated in the Lord's supper should not blind us towards the reality we experience in this world. We are committed to work towards this reality of the Lord's supper and its conditions (i.e., social, political and economic justice, §20).

3. Unity is given in Christ. Therefore he invites Christians to commun- ion. We understand "unity" in the sense of "reconciling differences" and we think that theological definitions might help for clarification. But theological disagreements should not keep us from celebrating the Lord's supper together.

We experience the presence of Christ in Spirit in different ways. Therefore we cannot speak of the Lord's supper as the "central act of the church's worship" (§1). Even in the proclamation of the word do we experience the fullness of the presence of Christ.

We share the opinion that Christ invites us to the table and that the Lord's supper is not the "invention or the property of the congregation" (§§ 9 and 20). But from this does not follow, according to our understanding, that the chairmanship of the celebration of the Lord's supper must be tied to the "ordained ministry" (§ 29). Every baptized and by the congregation commissioned member may chair the celebration of the Lord's supper.

IV. Ministry

1. We are happy to see that this section of the convergence statement begins with a description/presentation of the call of the whole people of God. In this description/presentation the differing views of the denominations are felt and yet it is not a complete levelling of views. However, it is surprising that the following declarations say little about the life of the people of God but instead speak a lot about the "ordained ministry".

We have difficulties with many of the statements on the ministry. However, we agree that there are special services (*Ämter*=Offices), appointments and also persons with special functions in the church of Christ. But we cannot agree with decisive statements of the declaration concerning the office/ministry. According to our understanding, the office is not "constitutive for the life and witness of the church" (§ 8). Furthermore, we do not regard a commissioning from within the congregation as being one for life with necessity. Similarly, we have no reason to think that the Spirit of God is necessarily connected with the office; the church of Christ can only pray that this is so. The importance which the office receives in the statements of the Lima document creates another difficulty for us. For it leads to an under-estimation, if not a surbordination, of the role of the "laity". The role of women within the people of God is unsatisfactorily described, as well (§ 18). Although we recognize that there are functions in the church which the congregation delegates to individuals, we nevertheless feel we must point out that this does not lead to the authoritative form of ministry as it is described in the convergence statement.

Persons with special functions live just as much in discipleship as all other Christians. The formulation of the text in § 11 according to which they are "representatives of Jesus Christ to the community" seems to be exaggerated in our eyes. However, we see that there is a connection between the understanding of ministry in the convergence statement and the strongly emphasized thought of the apostolic succession. Nevertheless, this does not convince us that the apostolic succession is of great importance for the church.

For us it is important, as well, to describe the continuity in the church of Jesus Christ. But this continuity lies according to the experience of the church in the gospel itself, as the scriptures testify. For again and again it proves itself as the living, shaping, and inspiring word. Although we do not know the apostolic succession in our church, we nevertheless share in the faith in God and in discipleship as members of the body of Christ.

2. It becomes evident precisely in the consideration of the convergence statement concerning the ministry, how difficult it is to bring the churches of different traditions closer together, never mind to achieve a visual unity. So we come back to our suggestion mentioned in the first part of our response to the Lima statement, i.e., to reconsider the concept of the unity of the church. To which unity does the Faith and Order Commission want to lead the member churches of the World Council of Churches?

CHURCH OF CHRIST IN ZAIRE
(COMMUNITY OF DISCIPLES)

In November 1985 the Administrative Council of the Community of Disciples within the Church of Christ in Zaire adopted the following resolution: "Since the time we have received the document on 'Baptism, Eucharist and Ministry' the members of our Community have been eager to study this document. Because of this and after discussions and deliberations, all the members of the administrative council, which consists of pastors and lay people, have given a positive response concerning the application of this document; and this the more so because these sacraments are always exercised in our Community since its birth, following the teaching of the New Testament."

● 650,000 members, 250 parishes, 230 pastors, 67 evangelists, 1,002 catechists.

METHODIST CHURCH — JAMAICA DISTRICT

Editor's note: The following is a provisional and personal account of discussions on BEM in this church.

The members of the Faith and Order Committee of the Jamaica District Synod of the Methodist Church have been having some discussions on the "Baptism, Eucharist and Ministry" document over some period of time.

There is general agreement over the main points of the document. However, there has been much discussion on the matter of second baptism by immersion. Some of the members request this. But this may be due largely to not being adequately informed of the teaching of the church when the matter is discussed with them.

The section on ministry creates an enigma for the church with regard to the acceptance of ordination for deaconesses. Their ordination does not include the word and sacraments. However, a dispensation may be obtained from the conference to administer the sacraments. Neither are they automatically recognized as clergy if they wish to function in that role permanently. Yet they are called upon to function in ministerial appointments where the need arises. Some discussion for clarification is continuing in relation to the section *"The Forms of the Ordained Ministry"*, *A. Bishops, Presbyters and Deacons.*

• 19,500 members.

THE PROTESTANT CHURCH IN SABAH (MALAYSIA)

Editor's note: In a letter of 20 August 1985, the President of this church wrote:

As our church has only come into being during the last twenty years we thus far did not feel that we have to contribute to the learnings and teachings of churches of much greater age. Just the same I feel, having used the BEM document during our last district synods for clarifying our point on baptism, eucharist and ministry, that you might like to hear from us.

Enclosed you will find an abbreviated translation of BEM into Momogun, our language in the northern part of Sabah, Malaysia, and also the English translation of part of our constitution which renders in short our understanding of BEM, not as document but what baptism, eucharist and ministry in our church means.

We appreciate this document as it gives us insight in the various understandings of churches, helps us to see our neighbouring churches in a new light and indicates that although those different views exist and will remain for some time, there is nothing theologically relevant which should keep us from working towards unity and united witness in our state. We certainly shall try to make the Lima document a point of discussion in one of the next meetings of the Sabah Christian Council.

The part from the constitution of the church, mentioned in the above letter, reads as follows:

3. The church is the communion of those who believe in Christ and who are on their way to the coming kingdom of God. The church receives its reality from its living worship and witness rather than from its institutions.

● 13,000 members, 7 parishes, 150 places of worship, 61 pastors, 200 lay preachers.

4. In holy baptism, God attests his new covenant with man. Whosoever has heard God's call and responds to it can receive baptism, and the children of those believers may also receive this sign of God's grace.

5. In the holy communion the church remembers what Christ did for his people on his way to the cross. The holy communion confirms them in their salvation, strengthens them in their lives and joins them together for future service.

6. This church believes Jesus Christ to be the one and only Lord and leader of the church. He guides his people whom he endows with manifold gifts through the Holy Spirit. Although the propagation of the gospel and the witness for Jesus Christ are the task of every member of the church, this church accepts the regular ministry as a proper means for administering the word of God and the sacraments. The ordained ministers are assisted by the lay helpers who are continuously trained and take a full share in administering the word of God.

THE THEOLOGY COMMITTEE
OF THE NATIONAL COUNCIL
OF CHURCHES IN KOREA

Introduction

The Theological Committee of the National Council of Churches in Korea had consultation meetings on 22 April 1986 and 20 May 1987, on the document "Baptism, Eucharist and Ministry" (BEM) of the Faith and Order Commission of the World Council of Churches. The purpose of the consultations was to study the document and to examine the implications for the Korean churches in their liturgical and ministerial formation. The committee has given particular consideration to the possibility and the necessity of promulgating the document in order to give challenges for the liturgical and ministerial renewal of the member churches in Korea.

1. General remarks

1-1. First of all, we want to express our thanks to the Faith and Order Commission of the World Council of Churches for their commitment and effort of more than fifty years to produce and promulgate such an important document which has found the common consensus among the various ecclesiastical traditions. As we look back on the long history of Christian churches, denominations were not always in agreement on all issues at stake for the life of the churches. For example, even when the churches were able to come together to worship, they were in sharp disagreement on doctrinal issues. Even after doctrinal issues seemed to settle, the liturgical problem was brought up at the table of the Lord's supper. This is true, in fact, in the historical traditions of the Western churches, and especially in liturgical questions. With this in mind, it was natural for the Western churches to become deeply interested in the liturgical unity as expressed in the BEM document. It is our understanding that this document is a special effort to bring unity between the Western churches and Eastern churches in the historical context as mentioned above.

1-2. The main themes which this document has dealt with have been the basic issues which have divided the world churches. However, we notice that such effort is coming from the perspective of the first-world churches, and is focusing especially on the issues of the past history of Western churches.

The document does not speak to the desperate realities of the third world, nor indicate the responsiveness of the first-world churches to the rest of the world. It seems that the document is mainly concerned with doctrinal differences, and therefore shows very little concern about the divided and suffering world to which the church is to minister. Although we recognize that the document has widened the horizon of church unity in the world, and has expressed openness to the coming kingdom of God, as well as assuming that ministry is the product of the social situation and theological context, we must point out the weakness in the document's theological assertions in the lack of responsiveness to the realities of the third world.

Of course there is no unified form of third-world theology as such among the Asian, African, South American and South Pacific countries. Third-world theology is being formed with great variety according to individual social, cultural, historical and geo-political particularities. However, the common goal of third-world theology has been responding to the people's aspiration for a new world order to create and maintain peace, justice and freedom. The third-world theology has risen as a movement of liberation for the poor and the oppressed from their suffering in the unjust and oppressive structures. Spiritually and culturally, the movement of third-world theology was born out of the struggle for rediscovery of self-identity; self-identity which was crushed by the domineering Western religions and cultural influences. It should be pointed out that the document does not address these genuine, meaningful struggles of the theologians and the people of God in the third world.

1-3. In connection with liturgical practices of the Protestant churches of Korea, generally the common characteristic is rather non-liturgical, or free of liturgical forms due to the influence of the Pentecostal movement. The majority of Korean Christians tend to regard the action of being baptized and participating in the eucharist as part of the means to receive blessings. In light of this, we confess that in our situation the BEM document is of very little concern to most of the churches in Korea. Disregarding this situation, however, and continuing to discuss and implement the document is ignoring the third-world churches and imposing the theological agenda of the first-world churches on the rest of the people of God in the world.

2. On baptism

2-1. The document places emphasis on the "incorporation into the Body of Christ" (§6), the important aspect of being called into the discipleship of Jesus Christ seems to have been weakened. We agree that baptism is not only "a sign of the kingdom of God and the life of the world to come" (§7), but also a call to serve for the kingdom. "Incorporation into the Body of Christ" is an internal experience for individual Christians. But from the perspective of the third-world Christian experience, it is a concrete and living response to the call of God to participate in the struggle of history and situation of the world.

2-2. Regarding the baptism of infants (§§11,12), there remain problems due to the difference in theological interpretation and respective church traditions. Particularly in our situation, an educational process for the parents who wish to administer infant baptism is still negligible. Thus, the importance of confirmation education ought to be emphasized.

2-3. It cannot be emphasized enough in the document that "baptism is an unrepeatable act", and that "any practice which might be interpreted as 're-baptism' must be avoided" (§13). Especially in the Korean situation this point must be emphasized to all denominational bodies. Due to the deep influence of dogmatic denominationalism, some churches are known to disrespect the baptism administered in other denominational churches and force "re-baptism" (§§15,16).

2-4. It is requested that a clearer theological decision and the question of the right to participate in the eucharist reserved only to the baptized be rendered. It is recommended that the right to participate in the Lord's supper be open to everyone who wishes to partake in it (comm. §19).

2-5. The BEM document recommends that baptism should normally be administered during public worship (§23). However, further discussions on baptism are suggested for granting permission for unavoidable occasions such as the case of a terminal patient where a private administration of baptism is a necessity.

2-6. In traditional religious practice, salt is sprayed as an act of exorcism and cleansing. In order to incorporate the traditional religious practice into the rite of baptism, there is discussion on the question of spraying salt as a symbolic act of cleansing before the administration of baptism.

3. On eucharist

3-1. In light of the Korean churches' past negligence about the eucharist aspect of worship services, it is a refreshing challenge given by the BEM document concerning liturgical renewal of the Korean churches in general. The document suggests that Korean churches strive to avoid divisions due to differences of eucharistic rites in various denominational bodies. We learned, however, that the division and schism of the Western churches was not particularly due to differing eucharistic rites, but because of political power struggles. If we can avoid the past mistakes, we can come to achieve unity on the liturgical matters of concern.

3-2. In the early Protestant mission era, there was almost a 25-year gap between the first baptism and the first administration of eucharist. This was perhaps because of the missionary misunderstanding about the Korean converts' lack of religious imagination. However, it is important to note that similar to the Christian eucharist, Korean people also used rice cake (Korean version of bread) and rice wine as basic elements offered and shared among the people in the traditional ancestor veneration rite. Thus, after the religious rite, a love feast was celebrated among the family, relatives, and friends of the family gathered together in memory of the venerated ancestors. It is encouraging to note in the document the meaning of eucharist is widened (§§ 22-26) and is also interpreted as communion of the faithful (§§ 19-21), allowing Koreans to indigenize eucharist as a "koinonia feast" into our traditional religious practices. The document has encouraged various theological efforts to interpret the eucharist in the traditional religious language and practice in order to create the indigenized forms of eucharist deeply rooted in the spirituality of the Korean people of God.

3-3. The most important and concrete meaning of eucharist today is, we believe, the sharing of food and the God-given nature together with the hungry and deprived people of the third world. It is hoped that the document will be mindful of this aspect of eucharist while the celebration of eating and drinking takes place in the midst of hunger, exploitation and destruction of human spirit and nature.

4. On ministry

4-1. On the meaning of Christian ministry, the document states that God calls all humanity to become God's people. Further, the church is called to proclaim and prefigure the kingdom of God. But the places and situations into which the church is called to minister are described in general terms. As a result, very little is said in concrete terms about how the church's ministry is to be performed in today's divided world of struggles for human rights, justice, peace and the integrity of life.

4-2. One of the major contributions of this document, with regard to the understanding of ministry, is a clear understanding of the ordained ministry in light of the calling of the whole people of God (§ 6). Where there is only a vague understanding of the theological reflection on the ordained ministry, such as in the Korean situation, a clear definition of the whole ministry of God's people in the document will stimulate the renewal of the theological understanding of the ordained ministry as such.

4-3.However, the document defines the role of the ordained ministry as "to assemble and build up the body of Christ etc." (§ 13), which ignores the role of enabling the mission of the church in the particular socio-political struggle of the God's people in the world. This narrow definition might encourage those in ordained ministry to be limited to the confines of the traditional parish ministry of the sort.

4-4. It is important to recognize the diversified forms of Christian ministry which have arisen out of varieties of cultural and historical contexts. However, such diversity is recognized only in the context of the development of the Western churches, and there is little mention about the diversity of various creative ministries being performed in the third-world situations which are worth our attention.

4-5. It is encouraging that the document opens the way for the ordination of women (§ 18) in an effort to renew the previously male-dominated structure of traditional ministry. This will stimulate various denominational bodies in the Korean churches to reconsider their limitation on the participation of women in the ministry of God in the Christian churches. The ordination of women in Korean churches is a particularly sensitive case where more than 70 percent of the congregation are women yet the ministerial structure is dominated and monopolized by the ordained male members of the congregation. Nonetheless, the BEM document mentions the twelve disciples of Jesus as the origin of the church's ministry which demonstrates that the document is not yet completely free from the patriarchal preoccupation of the majority of the churches of the first world.

4-6. For the division of labour of ministry, it is helpful to divide the forms of the ordained ministry into three parts: bishops, presbyters and deacons (§§ 19,20). However, clearer division and definition of the three forms is desirable, especially for the role of the deacons. It is suggested that the particular role of the deacons is to be liaison between the world and the church and to perform the prophetic role in the context of political, social, economic and cultural realities of the world today. It is recommended that the office of the ministry should be regarded not as status but rather as gift and talent, not as vertical authority but as horizontal solidarity, which would be flexible enough to meet the needs of the changing world.

4-7. The document clearly indicates that a distinction should be made between the "apostolic tradition of the whole church" and "the succession of the apostolic ministry" (Comm. § 34). Making this distinction seems to us to be a setback in the document and even a contradiction between the effort to maintain the traditional understanding of the ordained ministry and the effort to give a new interpretation of the ministry as the whole people of God involved.

We believe the apostolic succession should be applied to the whole people of God which forms the community of the faithful. Certainly the church itself is apostolic, as mentioned in the document (§ 34), and thus the whole people of God who are baptized into the ministry of Jesus Christ in the world can rightly be called "ministers". The document is inconsistent in this regard, making distinction between the apostolic tradition of the whole church and the succession of the apostolic ministry.

5. General evaluation and the future task

5-1. On the whole, the document clearly indicates an effort towards establishing basic unity of liturgical differences. On the other hand, by doing so it may lose the vitality and dynamic strength of the Christian liturgy in its diversity. There are some concerns which the search for unity and uniformity might create, thus creating further division and disparity.

5-2. Even though the BEM document clearly discerns the theological attitude of liturgy and its renewal in the churches, if it is not directly related to the life and realities of where we are located and performing our ministry, it has very little meaning. It means also that the function of the church is seriously called into question, when the baptism and eucharist and other liturgical forms are not concretely related to the life of the church and its people. The lack of reflection upon the meaning of church in the world today as the body of Christ is the main source of these questions. As a matter of fact, the churches in the West have lost the basic spirit and force of the Christian koinonia as they have structured the ecclesiastical system. The church, as we have come to understand, is the community of covenant between God and the people for the liberation of the poor and oppressed, which has been realized in the struggles of the Christian communities in the third world. In this struggle for the liberation of the whole people of God, we would certainly experience the dynamic strength of the meaning of life of liturgy of the churches.

5-3. In the light of these theological reflections, baptism would be interpreted as a response to the call of God and as a participation in the work of God for liberation of the world. And the meaning of eucharist would become clearer as an act of celebration in the process of such participation in God's work in the world. The ministry of the whole people of God will be found in this life of the worshipping community. Therefore, even without liturgies for baptism or eucharist, as we learn from the people in the Salvation Army, the life of work in the Christian ministry will be regarded as the important ingredient of participating in the liturgical life of the Christian communities.

5-4. We cannot escape from the realities of the world which is deeply divided in terms of race, sex, beliefs, nations, regions and ideologies. Despite these pressing facts, the document seems to show an illusory vision that unity will be easily achieved in the divided world today. While there appears to be some trace of discussion on the realities of the divided world today, these are not strongly reflected theologically in the document. In the situation of conflict and division, it is difficult and even hypocritical to confess that all are brothers and sisters at the table of the Lord. "If, when you are bringing your gift to the altar, you suddenly remember that your brother has a grievance against you, leave your gift where it is before the altar. First go and make your peace with your brother, and only then come back and offer your gift" (Matt. 5:23-24). If the document defines ministry as the calling of the whole people of the world, then the document must speak clearly to the current realities of the world in conflict, divided by race, sex, religion and ideologies. The document, however, does not face up to the realities of our divided world, but is preoccupied with the unity and uniformity of the liturgical formation.

5-5. The BEM document has contributed to the discussion of the liturgical renewal of the Korean churches as well as the question of opening up to more creative ways of indigenizing the Christian worship and liturgies in the traditional culture and religious practices. For example, in a funeral service, some ministers allow the family members to moan with loud voice as in the common people's practice. This is to make the whole liturgical movement more open and free to adapt the traditional culture and religious practices, in order to make them more acceptable for the people who expressed their feelings, joy and sorrows in the life of their religious rituals, Confucian, Buddhist and even shamanistic.

5-6. The future task of the Korean churches is to disseminate the BEM document among the member denominational bodies to bring about an ecumenical consensus on the liturgical renewal of the churches and to thus overcome the ills of denominationalism. The members of the committee have been challenged by the document to create an ecumenical book of worship in the near future.

Rev. So Young Kim
General Secretary
National Council of Churches
in Korea

Dr David Kwang-sun Suh
Chairperson, Theology Committee
National Council of Churches
in Korea

DATE DUE